Walking in Memphis

16 Historic Tours

Ron McDonald

Schiffer Publishing Ltd

4880 Lower Valley Road, Atglen, Pennsylvania 19310

Dedication

To my wife, Susan, who won me over when I discovered
that she, too, loved to walk and was filled with stamina.

Disclaimer: References to Paul Bunyan are pure flights of the author's imagination.

Schiffer Books are available at special discounts for bulk purchases for sales promotions or premiums. Special editions, including personalized covers, corporate imprints, and excerpts can be created in large quantities for special needs. For more information contact the publisher:

Published by Schiffer Publishing Ltd.
4880 Lower Valley Road
Atglen, PA 19310
Phone: (610) 593-1777; Fax: (610) 593-2002
E-mail: Info@schifferbooks.com

For the largest selection of fine reference
books on this and related subjects, please visit our web site at:
www.schifferbooks.com
We are always looking for people to write books on new and related subjects.
If you have an idea for a book please contact us at the above address.

This book may be purchased from the publisher.
Include $5.00 for shipping.
Please try your bookstore first.
You may write for a free catalog.

In Europe, Schiffer books are distributed by
Bushwood Books
6 Marksbury Ave.
Kew Gardens
Surrey TW9 4JF England
Phone: 44 (0) 20 8392 8585; Fax: 44 (0) 20 8392 9876
E-mail: info@bushwoodbooks.co.uk
Website: www.bushwoodbooks.co.uk

Other Schiffer Books on Related Subjects:
Memories of Memphis: A History in Postcards, 1-7643-2288-5, $19.95
Tennessee Ghosts, 978-0-7643-3118-3, $14.99

Designed by Mark David Bowyer
Type set in Souvenir Lt BT

ISBN: 978-0-7643-3564-8
Printed in China

Contents

Introduction

During the summer of 2006 my wife and two of our friends took a "holiday" to England to walk the Thames Path from Oxford and the Ridgeway National Trail. Despite my daily walks and runs and a number of backpacking hikes, I had forgotten how nice it is to walk all day long over easy trails and sidewalks from pub to pub, village to village, with soft chairs, chef-prepared meals, good conversation, and dancing and music waiting at the end of the walk. Finishing a run, showering, and dressing for work are one thing. Completing a day with a backpack on a wooded trail and setting up camp are another.

Walking for a day with a backpack and water to a public, relaxing location is special in another way. When you think about it, it's the best of both worlds — vigorous, endurance exercise during the day and the soft, easy life at night. It was also an obviously unique way to explore and enjoy highly populated areas. In fact, I enjoyed it so much I wanted to keep going.

Upon returning from England I immediately set off walking to the familiar places of Memphis. No longer on vacation I would begin very early, saving the longest walks for the weekends. Though I've been exploring Memphis on foot for twenty-five years, touring the city in the systematic manner we had just done in southern England was just as rewarding. Furthermore, I realized that these walks had long been my local sanctuaries.

A sanctuary is a place of peace, a refuge from the storm, a place to retreat from struggles to be revitalized and re-motivated. I have been building sanctuaries most of my vocational life. Not as an architect or designer, but as someone who offers people a counseling sanctuary, a musical sanctuary, a learning sanctuary, and an expressive sanctuary. I am a pastoral counselor, a musician and storyteller, a teacher, and a dance leader. The starting point for all my work is the creation of a sanctuary atmosphere where counselees, listeners, students, or dancers feel safe, serene, open, and grateful. I have always believed that when people arrive at such a special place where they exclaim, "This isn't Kansas anymore!", extraordinary experiences are at hand. Although it took me some time to recognize the connection between this walking and my vocational life, I now understand that this guidebook is really a sharing of the sanctuaries I know of in Memphis.

No city can be a good abode without its sanctuaries, and despite the fact that Memphis is a city many think of as dangerous, angry, and corrupt, it is, for me, as well as for many others, a place filled with beauty and hidden treasures. These sanctuaries are part of what makes Memphis a truly great city. In fact, they are probably central to its greatness, for they are inspiring, comforting, and extraordinary.

I invite you into these urban sanctuaries and offer this guidebook as an aid. Hopefully, it will add to the conversation, enhance the experience, and keep you, the walker, from getting lost. These hikes are what I consider the best walks in Memphis — I love them and walk them often — and I think you'll like them, too.

The Soul of Memphis

Walking in England is a walk through obvious human history. Walking in Memphis is, too, but it's not as obvious. Antiquity is ever-present in England. Everywhere you go there are ancient churches, castles, ruins — and *old, old* stories. In Memphis, though, there are only two known ancient places.

One is the Mississippi River, which, if you were to travel for miles along it, you'd soon realize that it's essentially the same today as it was in 1000 BCE. You get a little of that feeling walking along its banks in Memphis, for, as the saying goes, "The river is always the same and never the same." Ole Man River just keeps rolling along — you will feel its patience, serenity, and quiet power if you let it sink into your soul. I often think that part of the reason soul music has some of its origins in Memphis is because of the soul of the mighty Mississippi... It's deep, wide, and ancient.

The other claim to antiquity is the Chickasaw ruins represented by the burial mounds on the Fort Pickering river bluffs and Chucalissa Village Museum in T.O. Fuller State Park. These sites remind us that Memphis is much older than DeSoto's great conquest. People long ago found the protection of the riverbluffs, the richness of the soul, the abundance of animal life, and the mildness of the weather to be a great place to live and thrive.

Memphis is, indeed, about as close to the center of the nation as any city, and our diversity of people, cultures, and problems are about as American as apple pie. Sam and Dave, who recorded "Soul Man" at Stax Records in Memphis, might have said it like this: Memphis is a Soul City.

Mississippi River Barge

A Chucalissa Village sign.

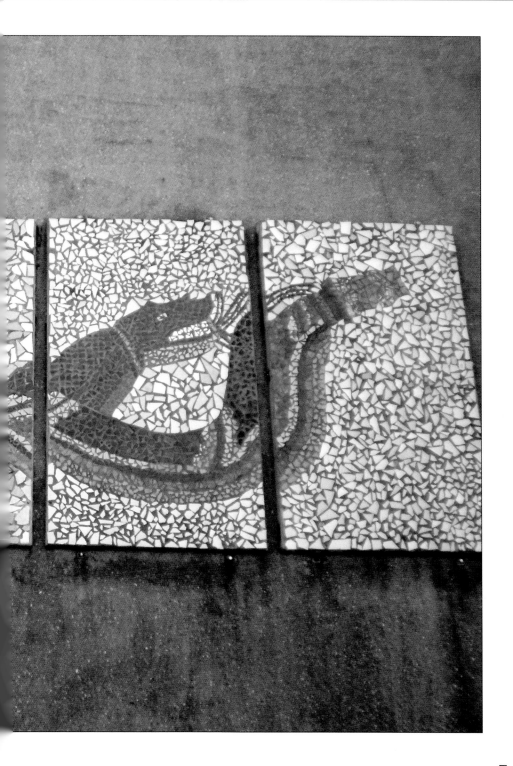

Contrasting History

The Slavery Era

Memphis' history is really most prominent beginning in the mid-nineteenth century — the antebellum South. There are three parks in Memphis that pay tribute to this era where slavery thrived and corrupted many, and those parks are right next door to places where African Americans and their cultural heritage were honored (Beale Street, Tom Lee Park, Southwest Tennessee State Community College).

The Civil Rights Museum reminds us of the awful days of Jim Crow. Concretely, so does the T.O. Fuller State Park; this was once a "colored park" while other prominent city parks were off-limits to "colored people" save on certain days. Memphis has long been a city where segregation was real and, while it is a part of our history that is often reviled by both whites and blacks, it still stands out.

Ironically, the majority of Memphians are African Americans and, while the African American culture is very strong here, the power and wealth is still concentrated in white enclaves. Though schools are now open to all races, there are only a handful of racially balanced educational institutions in Memphis: over ninety-five percent of the city's public school children are African American, which means that a majority of white children attend mostly white private schools. Racial history and polarities are involved in much of the ground Memphians walk on — as the entire city is a contrast between the underground cultural heritage rooted in black creativity and the white power elite.

After the Civil War ended slavery, Memphis remained a center for cotton trade, but the Yellow Fever epidemic in the late 1800s robbed the city of its luster for about twenty years. W. C. Handy, best known for his song "Memphis Blues," a testament to the former Mayor and political boss, E. H. Crump, had much to do with Memphis' revival, for he ushered in the popularity of the Blues. Meanwhile, Boss Crump kept the city organized and progressing, save for segregation, which he was instrumental in keeping alive and well in Memphis for the forty years prior to the beginnings of the Civil Rights Movement. That movement was enhanced by a young white singer, Elvis Presley, who grew up poor enough to be unafraid of African American culture, borrowing black rhythms and interpreting them in such a way that Rock and Roll was born in the "Home of the Blues."

Volintine-Evergreen

So much of Memphis is the history of contrasts and ambivalent sharing that those who embrace this assimilation feel richer and more whole because of it. Memphis' earthiness, or "rowdiness," as local writer John Branston calls it, can actually be a source of great inspiration. Some examples of this are listed below.

A typical Midtown home (Volintine-Evergreen) in un-typical Memphis weather.

McLean Baptist Church

Built in the 1950s by a staunchly segregated white congregation, McLean Baptist Church is today an integrated church in what is now a stable, mixed racial neighborhood — Volintine-Evergreen. In the 1960s, it was a place where racist "block busting" by unethical realtors were tearing apart the city by scaring away white residents with planted rumors of property values plummeting because "blacks are moving in."

Stax Records

Another example is found in the story of Stax Records, as told in what is now the Stax Museum (not included in these tours) or the Rock 'n' Soul Museum (which you will walk by). From this venue came some of the most creative and popular soul music in the world, and part of the reason for its success was that white and black musicians worked together as equals, despite being surrounded by Jim Crow laws and segregation.

The city's contradictions and transformations are, at the same time, both horrendous and inspirational. Somehow the better nature of Memphians rises above its brokenness.

What Walking Does for Us

In theology we often talk about immanence and transcendence. Immanence is the present, tangible world we live in. It is the ground we walk on, the earthiness of life. It's where we play and work. Transcendence is the sense of being up-lifted into a world beyond what we know. It is the world of the spirit where we experience the sublime. Transcendence is expressed through art, music, and worship, but we often find it inherent in the mundane world of nature. It calls us out of our daily routines — out into life beyond the usual, outside to walk on the road less traveled — where we can meditate and breathe in the spirit of life. Immanence grounds us; transcendence inspires us.

At its best, a walk takes us to where the birds and trees remind us of the inspiration of nature and where the art and architecture of humankind show us ways to aspire to be a better person. It is my hope that this book is more than fun. May it be an inspiration, but not just because of the natural beauty you encounter. May it also show you the city of Memphis' redemptive story — Memphis' history, lifted up throughout these walks, is a story of brokenness and healing and of how people who participated in bad things, when truly challenged, rose above what was wrong and corrected it. Though there are many cynical Memphians who think the city is fundamentally fractured and flawed, the stories featured in this book stand as a testament of the victory of goodness over evil, courage over cowardliness, beauty over ugliness. As M. K. Gandhi was quoted as saying in the award-winning movie, "When I despair, I remember that throughout history tyrants have had their way for awhile, but good always wins out in the end."

Martin Luther King, Jr. said in Memphis the night before he died, "Something is happening in Memphis." There's always been something happening in Memphis, and it has always been bad wrestling with good. Just as nature reclaims even abused land, recreating beauty where there was once desolation, Memphis' history is more about the history of creativity, goodness, and courage than abuse of power and oppressiveness. I hope this book might be a contribution to your sense of what life ought to be, not just the story of how it has been and certainly not just a nature walk.

A Tourist's Overview

If you are already a walker, then you don't need to be convinced that the best way to tour any location is on foot. Many walkers just set out as soon as they can to explore the city or countryside they find themselves in. These walkers hardly need a guide, as they will often find their own way.

What they won't find easily, though, are the almost secret places that only a few resident walkers know of. That is part of what this book is about. It is a guidebook from one special place to another — from places where some Memphians take their daily walks to places off the beaten path... Places where you can truly relax and see what is so special about Memphis. It's also a guidebook for seeing places in ways that most locals don't. In fact, most local residents don't even know the history behind some of these places, so walking and touring with this book in hand will make Memphis just that more interesting.

The Different Kinds of Walkers

This guidebook is designed for four kinds of walkers: the downtown tourist; the walker who wants to see Memphis without the need for a car; the walker who prefers to drive to designated spots, park the car, and walk; and the walker who wants to stay in hotels and take the bus to and from most of the walks.

• The **Downtown Tourist** could combine a few long walks with a number of tours that include the local museums and historical sites. This could be accomplished in a single weekend.

• The **No-Car Tourist** could take a bus into town, check into a downtown hotel, traverse all the downtown walks, and then walk to a Midtown hotel for the Midtown tours. After completing them, the no-car walker could then walk to an East Memphis hotel and tour that area. Then you could walk to another hotel further east and take in the Shelby Farms/ Germantown tours before taking a bus back downtown, or you might choose to walk most of the way on the new Greenline Trail. (It will be difficult to take in the state parks without a car to get you there, though.) The entire trek would take about a week.

• The **With-A-Car Walker** could stay in a hotel or at a friend's home and drive to the genesis of each tour. Certainly it would be the easiest way to traverse the miles of walking, but one might miss a few points of interest on the connecting walks. It could be accomplished in one week, or you could do it in two or three weekends.

• The **Walk-At-Your-Own-Pace Walker** will do this in sections, soaking it all in as he or she goes along.

• The **Bus Walker** will use public transportation to get to and from fourteen of the sixteen tours that start at one or more of the hotels along the way.

Mapping out the Walks

The Downtown Tourist

Includes two or three five-mile tours and lots
of moseying-type walking. Here is the schedule:

Friday: Check into a downtown hotel in the early afternoon, get settled, and visit a museum *(the Fire Museum, Magevney House, the Woodruff-Fontaine House in Victorian Village, the Cotton Museum, the Belz Museum, or Rock 'n' Soul Museum)*. Walk the Harbor Town Path before supper and then enjoy Beale Street, Grizzles basketball, or Redbirds baseball that night.

Saturday: If it's between May and October, walk to the *Farmers Market* and have breakfast, then (maybe) walk across the Old Bridge to the river bottoms in Arkansas and see the city skyline. Return across the bridge to the *Chickasaw Bluffs* and the *Metal Museum*, and then walk along *Martyrs* and *Tom Lee Parks* back to the hotel or to one of the local restaurants. In the afternoon, visit museums you haven't yet seen.

Sunday: Visit one of the historic downtown churches for worship services or pick a time between services to see the sanctuary. Between April and October, visit the Mississippi River Park on Mud Island in the afternoon and, if time allows, take one more walk along the Mississippi or walk half of the "controversial" walk to *Forrest Park* and *Sun Studio* before returning home.

Car-Less Walkers

In this tour, you'll be walking about
ten to fifteen miles a day.

Day One: Carrying only clothes and essentials in a backpack, begin at a downtown hotel, walking the *Harbor Town Path* alongside the Mississippi River. If it's between April and October, visit the Mississippi River Park on *Mud Island* and wade in the model river. In the afternoon, pick a few museums to visit and then spend the evening on Beale Street.

Day Two: Head south through the *Confederate*, *Tom Lee*, and *Martyrs* parks; maybe cross the Old Bridge over the Mississippi River. In the afternoon, walk through *Victorian Village to Sun Studio* and past *Forrest Park* to the *Church Health Wellness Center*. Afterwards, find a Midtown hotel to spend the night.

Day Three: In the morning, visit *Overton Park*. Walk through the woods and then visit *Brooks Museum* and the Zoo. In the afternoon, walk the *Evergreen* and *VECA Greenway* paths. Later, walk to *Cooper-Young* and enjoy the evening there.

Day Four: In the morning, check out of the hotel, walk through *Central Gardens* to *Christian Brothers University* to *Chickasaw Gardens* to the *University of Memphis* area and a nearby hotel. That afternoon or evening, walk the Galloway Park area, ending at a nice restaurant near Poplar Plaza.

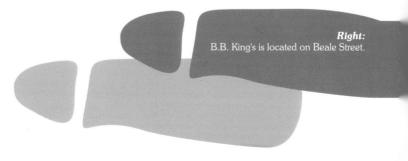

Right:
B.B. King's is located on Beale Street.

Day Five: Checking out of the hotel, walk through the *University of Memphis* campus to the *Audubon* and *Cancer Survivors* parks and the *Botanical Gardens*. After having lunch on Poplar Avenue, visit *Memorial Gardens* and then cross the interstate to a hotel near Baptist Hospital for a well-deserved rest.

Day Six: Check out of the hotel and walk the *Wolf River* trails, stopping midway to eat along Germantown Parkway. In the afternoon, walk through *Shelby Farms Park*. Returning, walk part-way on the new Greenline Trail, or just catch the bus along Walnut Grove Road to return downtown to a hotel for the night.

Day Seven: In the morning, take the bus to *Frayser* and get off at Rice Community Center in Frayser Park. Walk a five-mile loop through the residential hills of Frayser and then return to the community center to catch a bus back downtown. Transfer to a bus heading down Bellevue Avenue to Elvis Presley Boulevard, de-board, or drive to and walk the Whitehaven/Elvis Presley area, around the airport, and catch a bus back downtown to end the day.

Day Eight: Take a side trip to see the two state parks where Memphians picnic and play, but to do so you will need to rent a car. Drive to *T.O. Fuller State Park* at the southwest corner of Memphis and Mitchell streets; Mitchell turns west off of Third Street or Highway 61. The other park is north of Memphis — *Meeman-Shelby Forest State Park* — and is found by driving north on Highway 61 to Watkins Street (Highway 388); turn left (northwest), travel to the end of the four-lane road, and follow signs to the park's entrance.

With-a-Car Walker

With this tour, you have the luxury of picking *one* hotel
— downtown offers the best choices and best nightlife —
and traveling twice each day to the origin of each tour.

Day One: Begin by walking the *Harbor Town Path* alongside the Mississippi River. If it's between April and October, visit the Mississippi River Park on *Mud Island* and wade in the model river. In the afternoon, pick a few museums to visit and then spend the evening on Beale Street.

Day Two: Head south through *Confederate*, *Tom Lee*, and *Martyrs* parks, and maybe cross the Old Bridge over the Mississippi River. In the afternoon, walk through *Victorian Village* to Sun Studio, and then go past *Forrest Park* to the *Church Health Wellness Center*.

Day Three: In the morning, drive to *Overton Park*. Walk through the woods, and then visit *Brooks Museum* and the Zoo. In the afternoon, walk the *Evergreen* and *VECA Greenway* paths back to Overton and your car. Later, you might want to drive to *Cooper-Young* and enjoy the evening there.

Day Four: Drive to *Grace Saint Luke's Episcopal Church* and walk through *Central Gardens* to *Christian Brothers University*. In the afternoon, drive to the *Chickasaw Gardens* and then to *Poplar Plaza*. Walk the *Galloway Park* paths.

Day Five: In the morning, drive to the *University of Memphis* (do this early because finding parking is often difficult) and walk through the campus. Then drive to *Audubon Park*; be sure to visit the *Cancer Survivors Park* and *Botanical Gardens*. After having lunch on Poplar Avenue, drive to, and walk through, *Memorial Gardens* before returning to your hotel.

Day Six: In the morning, drive to Humphries Boulevard and park at one of the remote spaces near the Baptist Medical Center and then walk the *Wolf River* trails. Stop midway for something to eat along Germantown Parkway. In the afternoon, walk through *Shelby Farms Park* and then back across Wolf River to your car.

Day Seven: In the morning, drive to Rice Community Center in *Frayser Park* and walk a five-mile loop through the residential hills of Frayser. In the afternoon, drive to *Graceland* and walk the *Whitehaven/Elvis Presley* area around the airport.

Day Eight: For a side trip, drive to *T.O. Fuller State Park* at the southwest corner of Memphis and Mitchell streets; Mitchell turns west off of Third Street or Highway 61. The other park is north of Memphis — *Meeman Shelby Forest State Park* — and is found by driving north on Highway 61 to Watkins Street (Highway 388). Turn left (northwest), travel to the end of the four-lane road, and follow signs to the park's entrance.

Walk-at-Your-Own-Pace Walker

There is no reason why you can't divide up these walks. Do them in your own order and enjoy them in your own way (i.e. use them for getting into shape). Hey, it's a guidebook, nothing more!

If you do them all, you will have walked ten to eighteen miles a day — *that's 90 to 100 miles!* — and have toured Memphis in a way that most of the native residents have never done. These walks are a beautiful and fascinating tour.

Bus Walker

By using buses to get to and from tour origins and back to your hotel, you can easily plant yourself in one or two hotels for a nice evening's rest. It's easy to do this from a single downtown hotel, too, which would give you a wide variety of evening activities. If this interests you, read the section on "Public Transportation" in the next chapter. Plus, in Memphis the bus drivers are very friendly and helpful.

Walking Tips for the Tourist

Safety Advice

Memphis is a large city with major problems of poverty, powerlessness, addictions, and greed — the seedbeds for crime. However, though almost all Memphians and visitors do not experience crime, especially violent crime, some do. Only a fool walks through a major city without paying attention to a few safety rules. (The other strong words to remember are that if a crime happens to you, do not blame yourself in any way. Crime is the fault of the criminal, not the victim.)

While these tours avoid high crime areas, which means that you will miss out on some wonderful places that are like islands of peace and beauty in the midst of poverty and suffering, the areas recommended are not crime free. Stay on or close to the recommended paths and follow these simple rules:

1. **Stay aware of your surroundings** and walk away from suspicious places and people. This is the single most important safety rule. If you see the possibility of a crime occurring, you have a very good chance of avoiding it. Keep your eyes open.
2. **Walk strong**, and what I mean by that is walk in such a way that demonstrates that you *know* where you are going. Walk erect.
3. **Keep moving**, and be careful of whom you stop to talk with. If the person seems suspicious, acknowledge him, but *keep moving*. If the person has his hands in his pockets, keep your distance. Be civil to strangers, but don't worry about being polite.
4. **Morning time is the safest time**. Criminals usually operate in the afternoons and evenings, and especially late at night.
5. **Protect your life, not your things**. If you are accosted, give up your valuables. They can be replaced. If you must protect your valuables, don't carry them with you.
6. **Don't walk alone**. Though many choose to, walking in groups of two or more is much safer. Women, in particular, should not walk alone in desolate areas, and though these walks are generally not in desolate areas, they are in quiet and sometimes secluded areas where a woman should not walk alone.
7. **Running helps**. If you are in an area where you are concerned for your safety, jogging helps. Joggers are not easy prey and don't invite attack. Furthermore, if you aren't sure, don't hesitate to run from potential trouble or a shady person. There are times to be polite, but not when you are scared or nervous.
8. **Don't stop for panhandlers**. Although almost all panhandlers are not dangerous people, not stopping and looking at them while saying "No, thank you" should be sufficient. Walk on.

Injury Free Walking

Nobody can exercise without suffering the occasional injury, but there are a few principles to follow for protection from injury. Most of these walks are on pavement, which can be hard on the body. However, the surface is pretty stable and predictable, unlike trails, so it's a trade-off. Trails threaten the ankles while the pavement can be hard on the joints. Neither is that hard on walkers, however, for walking is a relatively gentle form of exercise. These four simple rules should protect you from injury:

1. **Wear good shoes**. Good shoes make pavements not much different than walking on grass. They absorb much of the shock.

2. **Walk quietly**. This is the most important advice there is, for if you are soft on your feet — and therefore quiet — your body is not feeling much shock or pounding.

3. **Let your knees bend**. If you were a model on a runway, you might be advised to lock your knees to put a swing in your backyard, but gentle walking requires a knee that gives with each step, acting as a shock absorber.

4. **Stretch gently before you set out**. Stretch your calves, hamstrings, quadriceps, and back (extensions - bending backwards, the belly pushing forward; and flexes - bending over).

Memphis Weather

Summertime in Memphis is HOT and HUMID. Average highs are in the low 90s, but most non-rainy days are ninety-five degrees or above. Early morning the temperature usually hits the 80s around 8 a.m., rising close to 90 by 11 a.m.

Spring-time in Memphis is often rainy, but temperatures are usually in the 60s in the early morning hours and reaching up into the 80s during the day. There's hardly a place in the world with better temperatures and blooming flowers than Memphis in spring.

Fall temperatures are about the same as spring, and the weather is normally quite a bit drier. Trails in the fall tend to be a bit dusty.

Wintertime includes lots of clouds and cold rain, but very little snow (we average about four inches a year). After two days of rain, we usually see three to four days of sunny weather. The average high in January is about forty-nine degrees. It can be 65 one day and 25 the next. Most mornings in January include a mild frost. Winter in Memphis is really just before Christmas through January. It begins to warm up in February when the Forsythia and Daffodils begin to bloom. The only bad walking days in Memphis are during cold winter rains or ice storms.

Frankly, the best time to visit and tour Memphis are the months March, April, October, and November. The weather is nearly ideal (save for periodic downpours), the colors are vibrant, and special events are in full swing. No month is bad, however, for Memphis weather is mostly quite mild. While some people can't stand the summer heat, even that can be resolved by taking early morning walks. One warning, though — Memphians are notorious for cranking up the air-conditioning so high that if you get acclimated to the summer heat, you may freeze indoors and you'll need a long-sleeved shirt or sweater!

Public Transportation

Almost all of these walks can be accomplished entirely on foot, but two of them do require public transportation (the Frayser and Graceland/Airport tours) getting to and from. Two also require a car ride (T.O. Fuller State Park and Meeman Shelby Forest State Park), but with the first twelve of the sixteen walks, you don't have to use a car or bus.

However, if you prefer to stay the whole time in one hotel downtown, you can take two buses to and from each of the first twelve walks: the #50 Poplar Avenue bus and the #34 Union Avenue bus. The Poplar bus will take you to the Midtown and East Memphis tours, and the Walnut Grove bus will take you to the last two tours (Wolf River and Shelby Farms). Both buses begin at and return to the North End Terminal at 444 North Main Street (near the Pyramid). The Frayser and Graceland/Airport tours can be reached by taking buses #10 and #20 (directions are in the specific tour chapters).

Memphis Museums and Special Spaces

Museums and special spaces are mentioned throughout the tours, but here is a list of places you can easily visit along the way.

1. **Woodruff-Fontaine House, 680 Adams Avenue**: A mansion along the historic "Victorian Village." Admission: around $10; open Wednesday through Saturday, 12 to 4 p.m. For more information, call 901-526-1469.

2. **Magevney House, 198 Adams Avenue**: A mid-nineteenth century home museum. For hours and admission fee, call 901-320-6370.

3. **St. Peter's Catholic Church, 190 Adams Avenue**: This beautiful sanctuary is filled with Christian art. Admission is free. For more information, call 901-527-8282.

4. **St. Mary's Catholic Church, 155 Market Street**: This beautiful sanctuary includes a special grotto. Admission is free. For more information, call 901-522-9420.

5. **Calvary Episcopal Church, 102 North Second Street**: The oldest public building (and a beautiful church) in Memphis. Admission is free; you can ask for an escort at the reception desk at the east entrance or call 901-525-0003 for more information.

6. **Mud Island River Park & Museum, 125 North Front Street**: Mississippi River Scale Model and History Museum. Admission to the park is free; museum costs under $10. Open April-May and September-October, 10 a.m. to 5 p.m., and June through Labor Day, 10 a.m. to 6 p.m. For more information, call 901-576-7241.

7. **Fire Museum of Memphis, 118 Adams Avenue**: Admission: around $6; open Monday through Saturday, 9 a.m. to 5 p.m. For more information, call 901-320-5650.

8. **National Ornamental Metal Museum, 374 Metal Museum Drive (Fort Pickering)**: Ornamental metal art and sculptures. Admission: around $5; open Tuesday to Saturday, 10 a.m. to 5 p.m., and Sundays, 12 to 5 p.m. For more information, call 901-774-6380.

9. **Cotton Museum, 67 Union Street**: Admission: around $6; open Monday to Saturday, 10 a.m. to 5 p.m., and Sundays, 12 to 5 p.m. For more information, call 901-531-7826.

10. **Belz Museum of Asian and Judaic Art, 119 South Main Street (Pembrooke Square)**: Open Tuesday to Friday, 10 a.m. to 5 p.m., and Saturday and Sunday, 12 to 5 p.m. For more information, call 901-523-2787.

11. **First Tennessee Mural and Art Gallery, 165 Madison Avenue**: Very impressive Tennessee theme art. Admission is free; for gallery hours, call 901-527-8981.

12. **Rock 'n' Soul Museum, 191 Beale Street (at FedExForum)**: Admission: around $10; open daily, 10 a.m. to 7 p.m. For more information, call 901-205-2533.

13. **Immaculate Conception Catholic Church, 1695 Central Avenue**: Beautiful sanctuary art. For more information, call 901-725-2700.

14. **First Congregational Church, 1000 South Cooper Avenue**: Inlaid Amiens Labyrinth. For more information, call 901-278-6786.

15. **Memphis Brooks Museum of Art, Overton Park**: Admission: around $10 or less (pay what you can on Wednesdays); open Wednesday and Friday, 10 a.m. to 4 p.m.; Thursdays, 10 a.m. to 8 p.m.; Saturdays, 10 a.m. to 5 p.m.; and Sundays, 11 a.m. to 5 p.m. For more information, call 901-544-6200.

16. **Memphis Zoo, Overton Park**: Admission: around $13; open daily, 9 a.m. to 6 p.m. For more information, call 901-276-WILD.

17. **Pink Palace Museum, 3050 Central Avenue**: Natural history museum. Admission: about $9; open Monday to Saturday, 9 a.m. to 5 p.m., and Sunday, 12 to 5 p.m. For more information, call 901-320-6320.

18. **Dixon Gallery & Garden, 4339 Park Avenue**: Admission: around $7; open Tuesday to Friday, 10 a.m. to 4 p.m.; Saturday, 10 a.m. to 5 p.m.; and Sunday, 1 to 5 p.m. For more information, call 901-761-5250.

19. **Memphis Botanical Gardens, 750 Cherry Street**: Beautiful gardens and an exceptional children's playground. Admission: around $5; open Monday to Saturday, 9 a.m. to 4:30 p.m., and Sunday, 10 a.m. to 4:30 p.m. For more information, call 901-576-4100.

20. **Cancer Survivors Park, Audubon Park**: Inspirational healing art and messages. This outdoor tourist attraction is open all day, everyday.

21. **Graceland Mansion, 3734 Elvis Presley Boulevard**: Elvis Presley's home, toys, and museum. Admission: $30-$70; open daily, 10 a.m. to 4 p.m. For more information, call 901-332-3322.

22. **Chucalissa Indian Village, T.O. Fuller State Park**: Ancient village grounds. Admission: around $5. For more information, call 901-728-3160.

23. **Stax Museum of American Soul Music, 923 East McLemore Street**: Although not included as a walk-by on these tours, it is a special place, similar to the Rock 'n' Soul Museum. Hours are 10 a.m. to 5 p.m., Monday through Saturday; admission is $12-15. For more information, call 901-942-7685.

This map is for both the Riverwalk and
Main, Beale, and Old Bridge Street tours.

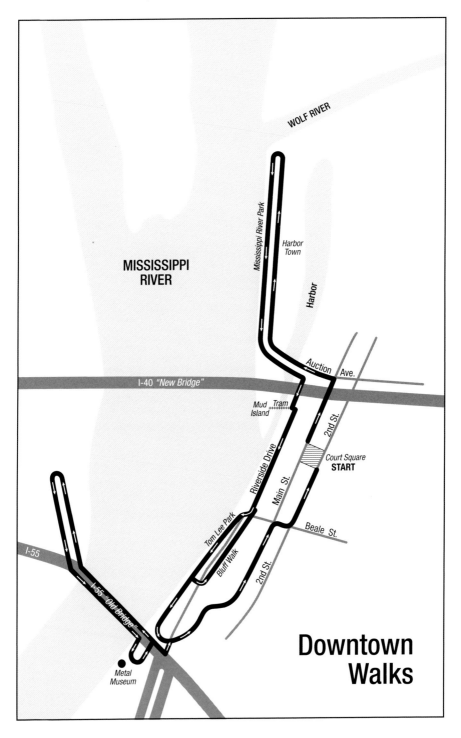

WOLF RIVER

Mississippi River Park

Harbor
Town

Harbor

MISSISSIPPI
RIVER

I-40 *"New Bridge"*

Auction   Ave.

Mud   Tram
Island

2nd St.

Court Square
START

Riverside Drive

Main St.

Beale   St.

I-55

Tom Lee Park

Bluff Walk

2nd St.

I-55 "Old Bridge"

Metal
Museum

Downtown
Walks

Touring Downtown
Riverwalk

Begin at Court Square and Main Street...
This tour is mostly along the Mississippi River. (7-9 miles)

Where to Stay

The Downtown is gaining hotels every year, and most of them are quite nice. Hotels recommended in this guidebook are rated by the website Expedia.

• **The Marriott**, at Main Street and Popular Avenue, is rated 3-1/2 stars.

• **The Crowne Plaza**, between Second and Third Streets, is rated 3 stars.

• **Comfort Inn** and **Marriott's Sleep Inn**, across from Court Square, is rated 3 stars.

• **The Peabody** is across from Autozone Park, near Beale Street. It's rated 4 stars.

• **Doubletree Hotel**, just off Beale Street, is rated 3 stars.

• **The Weston**, located across the street from FedEx Forum, is rated 3 stars.

The Tour

Beginning on Main Street near Court Square, walk north to Auction Street. This is the area known as the historical Pinch District, named after the poor people who lived here in the late nineteenth century and who were derisively referred to as "pinch-guts." It was a booming place when the Pyramid was hopping with events, but since FedEx Forum replaced the Pyramid, most of the commerce has moved south towards Beale Street. The Pinch is "pinched" right now, but it appears that the Pyramid will be revived as a Bass Pro Shop mega-center, which would positively affect this area.

The Downtown Trolley passes Court Square.

Auction Street

Sad Historical Footnote

Turn left (west) onto Auction Street. The small park to your left at this intersection has a historical marker noting that this was the general location of a slave auction, which just may be the most dehumanizing experience humans have ever created. It is hard to imagine how insensitive someone would have to be to see the anguish of a family being split apart by the sale of another human being.

Of course, slave owners and traders had been taught that black people were less than human and even happy in the state of servitude. A story is told of a slave at Andrew Jackson's estate, The Hermitage, in Nashville being told by a white man, "You slaves have it easy compared to those like me who live in freedom. I have to worry about feeding my family, paying for what I own, caring for my crops and animals, while you have but to work and everything is taken care of by your master." The slave nodded his head and softly replied, "That may be right, sir, but I would gladly trade places with you nonetheless."

Freedom might be one of the most fundamental desires of the human heart, and that particular slave's witty (and courageous) reply speaks for countless slaves who were humiliated by slavery and slave auctions. Such wounds take a long time to heal. The transmission of insensitivity to those who look and act differently, as well as the trauma of losing a loved one or becoming fatherless or motherless, can take a lifetime to overcome. It finally does when some determined generational victim of racism or the narcissistic abuse of power intentionally breaks the cycle, saying with one's life, "I will not let a victim psychology continue to take me down into poor self-esteem and rage," or "I will not let the racist attitudes of my ancestors determine how I relate to those who are different than me." When that happens, much change occurs. This happens often in Memphis where this racial wound is omnipresent. It is essential to the emotional health of this city and the whole South.

Sad Historical Footnote II

As you continue walking along Auction Street towards the Auction Street Bridge, to your right is a deep ditch that contains the Gayoso Bayou, which snakes its way under center city now. This was once the dirty water that allegedly bred the mosquitoes that spread Yellow Fever through Memphis in the late nineteenth century. So many people were stricken by that disease that thousands of people left Memphis, including many of its prominent citizens, professionals, and merchants. To this day some Memphians say that one of the main reasons Memphis has so much poverty is because of the "brain drain" that followed that tragic plague. Later in this tour you will see a monument to the martyrs who stayed in Memphis to minister to those who were dying during that sad time (at Martyrs Park).

Note: Both sides of the Auction Street Bridge have nice views of the old Wolf River Channel. To the right of the bridge is Harbor Town, an upscale residential area that is a primary reason why AARP recommends Memphis as one of the nation's ten best places to retire. You may leave the trail at any time to wander through this lovely area.

The Pyramid

The Auction Street Bridge is beside the Pyramid. Built in the early 1990s, it once was the arena home of the University of Memphis Tigers and the Memphis Grizzles. It also hosted many events, including Monster Truck shows.

Memphis, of course, is named after the ancient African city at the mouth of the longest river in the world, the Nile. Ancient Memphis is now Cairo, Egypt, located near the ancient Pyramids, memorials, and burial places of the great Pharaohs of Egypt, including Ramesses, whose likeness is preserved as a statue on the Memphis Pyramid's east side.

Critics of Memphis often comment that the Pyramid was the crowning glory of Memphis' infatuation with death. They say we have memorials for a dead civilization (the Confederacy) and a killing disease (the 1895 plague). Memphis is also where one of history's worst maritime disasters occurred (the 1865 explosion and killing of 1,000 Union troops on board the *Sultana* riverboat), and is the home of a dead rock star (Elvis), Martin Luther King, Jr.'s death place, and now a dead Pharaoh (Ramesses). When you think about it, all cities are infatuated with death, as they're all filled with memorials. According to Henry Wadsworth Longfellow, though, there is another way to view memorials, as indicated in a poem he wrote in 1838.

A statue of Ramesses the Great stands proud in front of a smiling Pyramid.

"Psalm of Life"

Lives of great men all remind us
We can make our lives sublime,
And, departing, leave behind us
Footprints on the sands of time;

Footprints, that perhaps another,
Sailing o'er life's solemn main,
A forlorn and shipwrecked brother,
Seeing, shall take heart again.

Memorializing the Good

What's unique about some of Memphis' memorials is that you have to look far beyond the horror of what they stood for (slavery, Jim Crow, terrorism — i.e., KKK) to discern what was good about them. Despite the obvious evil inherent in some human endeavors and institutions, underneath lies some level of nobility and dignity. If one had to be perfect to be honored or memorialized, then no one would be.

Throughout these walking tours, you will find memorials to heroes of a lost war, men who were blind to the evil they supported, and nostalgia for a time in which half of Memphis' citizens were treated like cattle at worst and second-class citizens at best. Their footprints are often not one we would want to follow, save for some of the redeeming qualities they possessed.

Nathan Bedford Forrest is a prime example of the contradictions of human nature. Memorials to him are on street names ("Forrest Avenue"), on a plaque downtown at Third and Adams streets where his business operated, and the controversial Forrest Park. He was an exceptional Civil War General, an astute businessman who owned slaves, and the founder of the Ku Klux Klan. Yes, he trafficked in slaves, fought on the side of the losers in a terrible war (fought for a terrible cause), and started a terrorist organization. Today he would be called a "warlord," but he also was a natural leader of men, uncommonly brave, generous with his time and money, and loyal to his view of his country and soldiers. Furthermore, he even attempted to disband the KKK after he saw how sadistic and evil it was becoming. He was not all bad, but many argue that the bad he favored far outweighed the good he sought to achieve.

Mississippi River Park

Just over the bridge, you'll cross Island Drive into the Mississippi River Park. There is a wide sidewalk on the topside of the park and a grassy trail down by the riverside. You will be walking 1-1/2 miles north in this park and then turning around, so choose either path. This is one of the most beautiful walks in Memphis... Maybe any of the nation's cities. The mighty Mississippi River quietly flows south, sweeping you along with its deep serenity.

Fifteen to twenty years ago the east side of this peninsula was storage ground for city work vehicles and materials. A century ago the peninsula was a small sandbar growing into what is now called Mud Island. Like all of the earth under Memphis, it is devoid of large stones. Digging is easy in Memphis, but someday there may be a dark side to this sandy loam soil.

About a hundred miles north of Memphis is the epicenter of the New Madrid Fault, home to moving earth plates that causes a massive earthquake about every three hundred years. The last great earthquake in this zone was in 1811, and it was one of the most powerful ever to occur in the states. It caused the Mississippi River to flow backwards, creating the beautiful Reelfoot Lake, now a state park, and making waves out of the sandy clay soil throughout this area of the south. Some Memphians think Harbor Town will be devastated by the next New Madrid earthquake, also a source of great controversy when the Pyramid was built, as many people wondered if its structural integrity would hold in an earthquake.

The *Annie Wepfer* tugboat on the Mississippi River.

Across the river is the state of Arkansas and some of the most fertile land in the world. Cotton, soybeans, and rice are major crops over there, and mosquitoes and water moccasins are abundant. There are a lot of mosquitoes in Memphis, but Arkansans think Memphis mosquitoes are nothing. Mosquitoes in Arkansas are reputed to have killed horses in their barns since they suck so much blood from them. It was the Arkansas mosquitoes that carried off Paul Bunyan's blue ox Babe's first calf, causing Babe to roll violently on the ground in grief. (Some say this was the real reason for the 1811 earthquake.)

At the north end of the park is a boat landing, and just beyond the upper level sidewalk is the old boat landing that falls steeply down to where the Wolf River empties into the Mississippi. This is the location where Tom Cruise's Mitch in the movie "The Firm" was subjected to the blackmail attempt by the law firm's security man, played by Wilford Brimley, which was meant to keep him in line with the crooked firm. Just above this old boat ramp is a wonderful small point with grass and a few trees... A place of real peace and beauty.

The Wolf River was one of those tributaries that used to be a garbage dump, where daily loads of trash was bulldozed into the river and swept downstream into the Mississippi and onto the Gulf of Mexico. Out of sight, out of mind — no, not quite, for the river used to stink. Fortunately, those days are long gone, and now the Wolf River is protected in many areas and is great for canoeing deeper inland. The Wolf River used to empty into the Mississippi through the Mud Island Harbor that was underneath the Auction Street Bridge, but it was rerouted to this terminus in the mid-twentieth century.

Turn around and again walk one of the two paths, this time going south. You'll see the Mississippi-Arkansas bridges; the closest one is the I-40 bridge, called by most Memphians "the new bridge." It's only forty years old. The old bridges further south are about one hundred years old.

The river fluctuates about forty feet a year. In July and August it is usually at least ten feet below zero (what is probably an estimate of the river's mean), which is about thirty feet below the grassy path. In March and April, the water sometimes rises over the grassy path, thirty-five feet above zero. When the river is that high, tributaries like the Wolf River are virtually dammed up and cause flooding in low-lying areas about five miles back. Such fluctuations remind us that the Mississippi River is a major force.

Its size, depth, and changing nature are also some of the reasons why there are so few pleasure boaters on the river. It is known as a dangerous river, filled with shifting currents and undertows, although some people suspect that the real reason there is little river play is because the river is still fairly polluted. It's not as bad as it used to be, but you won't hear ads from local restaurants that they serve Mississippi River catfish. Those who do enjoy the river, however, say that it's not unusually dangerous or polluted.

Note: When you return to the south end of the park, if you continue walking south, you will come to the entrance to Mud Island Park, which is open daily 10 a.m. to 5 p.m. April through October. Within this park is a scale model of the Mississippi River that is much fun to wade in and explore. It really gives perspective to the breadth of the river. However, you can skip the park for now and visit it later via the Mud Island tram bridge from downtown.

Elvis at the I-40 Welcome Center just across from Mud Island River Park.

The Elvis Station

If you choose to return to the Auction Street Bridge, take the opposite side of the bridge from when you came over it for a different view of the harbor. Just as you come off the bridge, scurry down the grass embankment into the Pyramid parking lot. It used to be a nice walk up the long ramp to the Pyramid and around it, but since the Pyramid was closed a metal gate blocks the walk-around route. So you will need to walk on the roadway just east of the arena. Continue south through the parking lot onto the access road. Just as you pass the old cement mixing facilities, turn right onto the grass and walk towards the river. You'll find a small gravel path that will take you to the back of the Interstate-40 Welcome Center. Inside are large statues of Elvis and B.B. King, lots of information on Memphis, and cold water and restrooms.

Ready for a Lunch Break?

There are a number of excellent restaurants one block east of Front Street on Main.

• **Alcenia's Deserts and Preserves Shop**, 317 North Main, is a lunch-only soul-food place where the owner, Alcenia, hugs each person who comes into her friendly restaurant.

• If you want old-time Memphis barbeque (sic) for lunch, **Leonard's**, at 100 North Main, serves heaping plates of it.

• Just across the street at 86 North Main is **Café Napoleon**, where an African American chef named Bruno serves some of the best Italian food in town.

Further south on Main Street are many more excellent restaurants. The oldest café in Memphis — where Hollywood often films its movies — is **The Arcade** at 540 South Main.

Jefferson Davis Park

Continuing south from the I-40 Rest Stop, or the Elvis Station, take a stroll through Jefferson Davis Park, named after the President of the Confederacy who lived for a short time in Memphis in his later years. You will be walking under the Mud Island Tram and Bridge. At the southern edge of this park, continue south on the sidewalk next to Riverside Drive. Above you is Confederate Park, which is guarded by World War II cannons; these replaced the Civil War cannons that were melted down for munitions during World War II.

These two parks have long been controversial in Memphis among those who argue that they honor bad values and a dark time in American history. This is one of those memorials where you have to look underneath the obvious evil of the institutions that supported slavery and the war in defense of slavery to understand the hearts of the men who are memorialized.

Jefferson Davis, whose large statue sits in the center of the park, will probably never be seen as a great American, but there is ample evidence that he loved his family, was loyal to his friends, and was willing to give himself to a higher cause that he thought was right. His tragic flaw, which was probably the tragic flaw of all the great Southern Civil War leaders, was that he was unable to understand the terrible evil of the foundational institution (slavery) that was a cancer to a whole nation.

Jefferson Davis in Confederate Park.

Tom Lee Park

Within a half mile of these memorials is a memorial of a black man, Tom Lee, whose heroic deed represents the hope for compassion's victory over the cancer of slavery and racism. To get there, walk south past the Memphis Mississippi River gauge, a long rusty metal strip that climbs from the sidewalk wall down to the river and what will soon be a recreational "Beale Street Landing" that promises to be a beautiful, restful place. Just beyond it will be Tom Lee Park, an oasis of green grass and small trees. Midway into the park is an obelisk, the original 1954 monument to Tom Lee, who, on May 8, 1924, saw the *M.E. Norman* steamboat, loaded with partying engineers, capsize fifteen miles downstream and paddled his small boat from struggling survivor to shore over and over again. In all, he saved thirty-two people from drowning.

Sculpture of Tom Lee saving a distressed man
by David Alan Clark... This might be the
symbol of hope for Memphis.

Just south of the obelisk is a bronze sculpture of Tom Lee saving a desperate man. Some people think that this striking monument is a symbol of the redemptive stories of Memphis. Such moral heroism will always be needed in any community, and Tom Lee Park, sitting less than a half-mile from the Jefferson Davis and Confederate parks, is a striking contrast and testament to the color-blindness of good deeds.

Perhaps this striking sculpture does represent hope for Memphis. A city racked by racial discord and a long history of injustice (like many Southern cities), it will probably take an African American person with a calm strength and determination to reach out to white Americans to pull the city from its capsized condition. It will have to be, though, an effort of love and compassion, not an assertion of power.

Tom Lee Park used to be a small slither of land between Riverside Drive and the river, but in the 1990s huge amounts of sand, gravel, and dirt were laid here to make this massive land larger. Today the park is home to the greatest expression of gluttony in the world: the Memphis in May Barbeque Contest. People dress up like pigs (literally), drink, dance, and eat, eat, eat. If you've got friends who invite you to their booth, it's a great festival and a wonderful place to gain weight and pack in the cholesterol. If you don't have friends there, though, you have to beg for food (not a problem for pretty girls), buy some at the vendors, or just walk around and watch people eat and drink from elaborate booths, surrounded by loud music. It may be a deadly sin, but it's fun!

Unfortunately, this also means that in late April through May the Tom Lee Park is closed to walkers and driving traffic for the Memphis in May festivities. If you are walking during that time, climb the stairs at the base of Beale Street just across Riverside Drive up to the bridge beside the park's entrance and take the upper Riverwalk. You won't be able to see much because of the temporary fences, but before long you'll be in the Riverbluff residential area, where you can follow the Riverwalk signs to the bridge back across Riverside Drive into Ashburn Park. Otherwise, walk through Tom Lee Park to the hill on the south side of the park that also leads to Ashburn Park. The view from Ashburn Park might just be the most spectacular on-the-ground view in Memphis.

To the right of Ashburn Park you'll see the continuation of the Riverwalk, flanked by a condominium that used to be the Holiday Inn flagship hotel. Holiday Inn was established in Memphis in the 1950s by Kemmit Wilson, who saw the need for a predictably comfortable motel chain and made millions from it.

Martyr Park

This path leads to Martyr Park and a monument to the heroes who ministered to those suffering from Yellow Fever in 1895 (there were earlier Yellow Fever epidemics in Memphis, too). This disease was traced to the Gayoso Bayou, which, in the late nineteenth century, was a cesspool of waste and a breeding ground for disease-bearing mosquitoes. The martyrs memorialized here were the few brave souls — many of them nuns — who stayed behind to care for the sick while many fled Memphis. As a result, a number of these heroes and heroines also died from Yellow Fever.

This great tragedy sickened the city in more ways than just the physical, for the massive loss of population — the brain-drain — and accompanying loss of city revenue was part of the reason why Memphis ended up bankrupt and had to surrender its corporate charter soon afterwards. You could compare it to a flood or hurricane in the toll it laid on the city. Some Memphians point to the brain-drain of that time as having a still lingering effect on the city, although that's hard to substantiate when you look at the excellent educational and medical institutions that Memphis is now famous for.

Memphis' Martyrs Monument in Martyrs Park.

The Returning Loop

Just beyond the Martyr's memorial, the Riverwalk ends in a small loop where you must turn around for the return journey. Just beyond this loop is the Unitarian Church on the River, probably the most popular wedding chapel in Memphis because of its gorgeous view of the Mississippi River. It is also an oasis of liberal theology in a mostly conservative Bible-Belt city.

After returning to Ashburn Park, take the bridge across Riverside Drive and walk through the Riverbluff residential area, following the Riverwalk signs. Within a half-mile, you will be back on the bluff overlooking the river. Going north on this section is a constantly beautiful

view until you descend down to Riverside Drive along the steel and wooden bridge that begins at Beale Street.

Stay on the east side of Riverside Drive until you reach Court Avenue and the stairs up to Confederate Park. Climb those stairs and walk through Confederate Park — there are some interesting markers on southern history and a Ten Commandments Monument — to Front Street. Go a block north on Front Street and turn east (right) onto Adams Avenue. The City and County Offices are the large white building on your left; the Hall of Mayors is on the ground floor.

The "New Bridge" (I-40) and the Pyramid, as seen from the Arkansas side of the river.

Places of Worship

Calvary Episcopal Church

One block further east at Adams Avenue and Second Street is Calvary Episcopal Church, the oldest public building in Memphis. If you ask, the receptionist at the east door will let you into the sanctuary to experience the ambience of this beautiful church.

Calvary was one of many struggling churches during the Downtown's decline in the 1970s, but in the early 1980s they hired a rector, the Rev. Doug Bailey, who had the charisma and determination to convince the church to open wide its doors. Ministries to the homeless, addicts, families, gays and lesbians, downtown workers, as well as its long-standing worship and musical tradition, made Calvary into one of the strongest liberal churches in the city.

Calvary is complemented a few blocks away by the Union Mission ministry to the homeless, which is supported by the area's conservative churches. Union Mission feeds and houses hundreds of homeless and addicted men and women each month in return for their participation in worship, including listening to a sermon and call to Christ. Calvary's liberal approach to helping struggling men and women and Union Mission's conservative approach are united in their loving concern for some of the most disrespected and neglected people in Memphis. This commitment to ministry to the downtrodden fosters a level of respect between the denominations that is not evident in theological discussions.

Right:
A statue of Columbus is located on the east side of Calvary Episcopal Church, the oldest public building in Memphis.

48

St. Peter's & St. Mary's Catholic Churches

Just across the street from Calvary is St. Peter's Catholic Church. Inside is one of the most beautiful sanctuaries anywhere, filled with sculptures. One of them, a very large crucifix, was originally donated to Calvary Church, but they didn't like it. They told the parishioners at St. Peter's that they couldn't get it in the front door, so St. Peter's took it and hung it on one of

the front pillars. It remained there until the church was remodeled in 1982; now it hangs on the wall of the east wing of the cathedral. It is massive, and some might think it's beautiful.

Four blocks north of St. Peter's at Market and Third streets is St. Mary's Catholic Church, which just may be the most beautiful sanctuary (and a striking Grotto, a sacred cave or inner chamber) in the city.

Saint Peter's Catholic Church.

The Gold Buckle of the Bible Belt

Memphis is the gold buckle of the Bible Belt. There are more mega-churches here than almost anywhere else in the world. Though Calvary Episcopal Church has a membership of over 1,000, it is dwarfed by the Mississippi Boulevard Christian Church, midtown's giant, and the downtown giants, Monumental Baptist and Temple of Deliverance, the mother church of the Church of God in Christ.

However, the really big churches are where the big parking lots are in East Memphis, including Bellevue Baptist Church (30,000 members).

Mud Island Park

Two blocks back to the west of St. Peter's Catholic Church, just to the north of City Hall, is the Mud Island Walkway above the Tram deck. The Tram ride is relaxing, but the bridge walk lets you mosey along above this bird's eye view of the Mud Island Harbor. This long covered bridge to the park is a wonderfully peaceful walk, although its real claim to fame is a scene from the movie, "The Firm." In this scene, an evil looking, white-haired man is running above Tom Cruise's character Mitch as he stands pensively in the Tram, unknowingly stalked by this man bent on killing him.

Mud Island Park is a lovely place. You might want to stay for a long time, so, if it's late, you might want to save this short but slow walk for another time. The park is only open April through October, though.

The bridge ends just above Mud Island's scale model of the Mississippi River. Go down the stairs and you can walk south again along the river, wading in the water. It is a fascinating Riverwalk, which really acquaints you with the immense scope of the Mississippi River. Water from nearly two-thirds of the continental United States empties into the Mississippi and flows peacefully down to the Gulf of Mexico.

This whole park is a Memphis oasis, a jewel of a place, but grossly under-used. You could easily spend the better part of a day here, boating, wading, eating, relaxing, and visiting the wonderful Mississippi River Museum. When you return, you may continue walking north out of Mud Island Park onto the Island Park where you began or you could re-cross the Tram bridge back to Main Street and return to your hotel.

Mud Island River Park from Riverside Drive looking across the harbor. This is the highest you'll ever see the Mississippi River.

Main, Beale, and Old Bridge Walk

Begin at Court Square and Main Street. View downtown museums, entertainment, art, and the Arkansas bottomlands. (5 to 10 miles)

The Tour

Begin this walk on Main Street at Court Square. This park has just been remodeled. It took them two years to do it (our taxes hardly at work) — a job two men with hand tools could have done in a year or less. At least they didn't ruin it; it's still a nice centerpiece for the Downtown, showing up often in movies filmed in Memphis.

The centerpiece of Court Square is the fountain. In 1895, a boy fell into its murky waters and, as dumbfounded people watched, drowned. Their inaction was scandalous and received scathing words in the local paper the next day. Evidently, people's apathy and paralysis was as alive and well in the nineteenth century as it is today.

After wandering through Court Square, head west to Confederate Park. If you didn't check out the monuments there on the earlier tour, here's your second chance. They're very interesting.

Front Street

Confederate Park is on Front Street. Continue walking south on Front Street. This area is under consideration for redesign so that the view of the old Wolf River Channel and the Mississippi River are more accessible to the public. The argument is that this prime street is improperly used for public services like the post office, fire station, and the under-used library. They could be torn down, although the old post office has been remodeled into part of the University of Memphis Law School and may be the cornerstone of this re-developed section of the Downtown.

Front Street continues south for over a mile, where it comes to the pavilion at the Saturday morning Farmers' Market. Above it is Central Station, the Amtrak station, where the famous "City of New Orleans" train stops on its way between New Orleans and Chicago. Arlo Guthrie made this train famous with his hit folk song, "Riding on the City of New Orleans" — another of the two hundred or so hit songs with Memphis mentioned in the titles ("Changing cars in Memphis, Tennessee"). You can see the train between 6:30 and 7 o'clock every morning. Just beyond the pavilion Front Street ends at Calhoun Street; turn right and walk to Riverside Drive.

Tennessee and Arkansas Bridge

Warning! The walk over the I-55 bridge — the Tennessee and Arkansas Bridge — can be unnervingly noisy and bone-rattling. It's not for everyone. The trucks are frighteningly close. If, however, you love adventure and like to walk where others dare not tread, this is an unforgettable trek — great heights, historical bridges, and a serene river bottomlands with an incredible view of the Memphis skyline.

If you don't like rough walks, skip this one and go under I-55 just before it becomes the bridge. Check out the Ornamental Metal Museum and the Indian burial ruins, and then return to Riverside Drive to Calhoun Street and Central Station.

For the more adventuresome, go south on Riverside Drive and turn right onto the entrance to I-55. Stay on the grass near the fence (really a hedge) near the railroad tracks that are on the right; this will take you within 150 yards to a sidewalk next to the last exit before the bridge. If you go under the interstate here and then up the steps, you'll be on the south side of the bridge — *facing traffic* — as you cross the Tennessee and Arkansas Bridge. At the bridge's southeast edge is a poem by Walter Chandler, who was mayor of Memphis for two terms in the 1940s and 1950s.

The "Old Bridge" (I-55) from Fort Pickering and the National Ornamental Metal Museum grounds.

Build we better than we know,
Who span the mighty stream below,
Who join the shores of neighbor states,
And open wide the friendly gates.
Who strive to clasp the outstretched hands,
To bind fore'er our native land.
To link the east with golden west,
And share with all the nation's best.
We stir the hearts of conquering youth,
And spread the word of God and truth.
We serve the busy marts of life,
And draw mankind away from strife.
We cross vast acres fresh and green,
To reach the oceans few have seen.
To view the mountains white with snow,
And know man's blessings here below.
And for the coming years to see,
With things unknown and yet to be.
Now pray we all with one accord,
Now bless this bridge, O Gracious Lord.

The bridge, completed in 1949, is 1-1/4 miles long. Over the last quarter-mile you are about six feet from traffic, separated by a knee-high concrete barrier. It's unnerving, but it ends soon, just above old Highway 70. From there you can walk down the embankment to the gravel road and go under all three bridges into the river bottomlands.

The View from Arkansas

As you walk north, it becomes refreshingly quiet. These flatlands of Arkansas have a serene, relaxing beauty about them that grows on you the longer you're in them. Every few years in the early spring, this farmland, split by the gravel road you are on, floods, but if it's dry after you've walked a half-mile, the view of the Memphis skyline is terrific. You'll feel like you're in a different world — like Dorothy's first view of Oz in "The Wizard of Oz."

The soil around you is some of the richest in the world. West Memphis and beyond is mostly protected from flooding by levees, but this area still gets totally submerged at least once every three years, leaving silt and nutrients behind that feed the soil and keep it flat as a pancake. Before the levees, floods used to drift for miles, feeding soil, leveling the ground, and keeping the population sparse. This whole southeastern section of Arkansas is terrific farmland — rice and soybeans are in great abundance around here. If the soil is muddy, it becomes as sticky as peanut butter and is called "Mississippi Gumbo."

West Memphis, Arkansas, the town just over the levee to the west of where you are, is a *flat, flat* town that's long been a major truck stop at the junction of I-55 and I-40. Some think the city motto ought to be "West Memphis: A Good Place to Get Gas." Especially if you eat at Ponchos on Highway 70 near the second exit off of the I-55 bridge; Ponchos has been a favorite Mexican restaurant in eastern Arkansas for years.

The Memphis Skyline from Arkansas and the Mississippi River bottoms.

Another Bridge

When you've decided you have walked far enough, turn around, go up the embankment on the north side of the bridge, and re-cross the bridge from the north side. This has a view of the two railroad bridges. The one nearest you used to also be the automobile bridge that was constructed with six by six planks across a steel platform (which you can see if you walk along the old highway bridge entrance to the Tennessee and Arkansas Bridge entrance).

Once again this bridge walk is VERY noisy. Hopefully, though, the serenity you gained down in the river bottoms will make it tolerable. You can use the time to practice your yodeling (a form of singing invented by Paul Bunyan while vacationing in the Alps), and if you are afraid of big trucks, this would be the place to overcome your fears!

This was the original roadway across the Mississippi River from the Arkansas side.

Main Street

Ornamental Metal Museum

After leaving the bridge, visit the Ornamental Metal Museum, which is off to the right (follow the signs) and across the street from two old Indian burial mounds. Here is one of Memphis' most spectacular river views. The mound just across the street from the museum was hollowed out at the top so it could be used as an artillery redoubt during the Civil War. Originally it was a Chisca Indian mound.

National Ornamental Metal Museum gate, looking towards a Civil War redoubt dug into an Indian burial mound

Afterwards, retrace your walk to Riverside Drive and then to Calhoun Street to the terminus of Front Street. From there, take the small road that turns southeast (south of the Farmers Market) to the train tracks. Cross the tracks and turn back north onto the Amtrak train platform. When you get to Central Station, walk through what you can of the station, which is now half depot, half banquet space. Such old depots are a step back in time. Exit onto Main Street and walk north.

A half-mile north on Main Street and you are in the South Main Art District, beginning with D'Edge Gallery, just south of the Arcade and adjacent to Central Station. Named for its owner, Deborah Edge, it has a nice collection of one of Memphis' finest African American artists, George Hunt.

National Civil Rights Museum

Walking north, just east of Main Street, is the old Lorraine Motel where Martin Luther King, Jr. was assassinated. Now the National Civil Rights Museum, this is one of the most stirring locations in Memphis. The museum is very emotional and enlightening.

Before the Museum was created, a person could walk into the original King room by asking the front desk clerk for a key to the room. On the wall were pictures, mostly cut out

from old *Life* and *Look* magazines, of the tragic event. One minister, who had just visited Graceland, paying big bucks to see Elvis Presley's home (where, at the time, Elvis' death by drug overdose was glossed over), said upon seeing the simple display for free in the Lorraine room, "It must be that the pseudo-truth is expensive, but the real truth is free."

Lorraine Motel was where Martin Luther King was assassinated in 1968. The guard on the roof is watching out for the 2009 visit of the Dalai Lama.

63

Beale Street

Memphis' Soul Music

When you arrive at the Orpheum Theater, you will be on Beale Street. Turn right. For the next two blocks you can enjoy the soul music of Memphis, framed by statues of Elvis Presley and W. C. Handy. The only time this street is half-way quiet is in the early morning light. At other times, especially at night, it's an exciting place to be — crowded with people, pungent with the smell of food, and music playing everywhere. Most nights include impromptu street gymnastics by the Beale Street Flippers, a group of young men and boys who perform flips for tips.

Beale Street is known as the "Home of the Blues," and in the middle of the open-air performance park is a statue of W. C. Handy, whose Memphis home is the small house at the eastern edge of this district. Known as the "Father of the Blues," during Handy's fifteen years in Memphis in the early twentieth century, he organized a very large Blues band that crossed racial lines. His sheet music on the Memphis Blues and St. Louis Blues were big national sellers. No doubt, his creativity, organizational, and promotional ability changed American music. Blues and jazz are perhaps the quintessential American music genres, and Handy is a main reason why Memphis claims it as the "Home of the Blues."

Elvis statue on Beale Street

Beale Street statues: Elvis...

... and W.C. Handy,
Father of the Blues.

Memphis' Sports Pride

Next to Beale is FedEx Forum, home of the Memphis Grizzles and University of Memphis Tigers, the pride of Memphis. Despite the lure of baseball and football, Memphis is really a basketball town, producing the best basketball players of any city in the world. North Carolina and New York City don't even come close. Memphis basketball players are so good we could easily field even our weakest high school team and beat Michael Jordan in his prime. No one in Memphis doubts that! Just think of how little chance Jordan would have against the mighty Tigers or the Grizzles. Someday the Tigers are going to win the national title and the Grizzles are going to be the NBA champs. In the meantime, we'll settle for knowing that Jordan is no contest against any of our teams.

Third Street

When you're ready to leave Beale Street, go to Third Street, walk north to the first-class Peabody Hotel and take a short stroll through the first floor. If you are there at 10 a.m. or 4 p.m., you can see the famous Peabody ducks waddling along the red carpet between the lobby fountain and the elevator where they spend their days in the pool surrounding the fountain. At one end of the lobby is a player piano. When the mechanism isn't playing the piano, John Boatman, one of Memphis' most creative and under-appreciated musicians, is. Be sure to say hello to him!

Autozone Park

Back out to Third Street and Union Avenue, cross the street to Autozone Park. At the entrance is a statue of Paul Bunyan at bat. Of course, he was just a boy then. At every game, opposing coaches, suspicious of his age, asked to see his birth certificate for verification. Alas, since his bat was big enough to cover the whole strike zone, all they did was walk him, which caused Paul to lose interest in baseball and become a woodsman instead.

Most of the time you can walk into the stadium and view one of the finest small professional ballparks in the nation. Completed in 2000 (the year Albert Pujols hit the homerun that won the Pacific Coast League Championship), this is the home of the Memphis Redbirds, a Triple A farm team of the St. Louis Cardinals. Fans are treated so nicely, and the baseball is good enough, that attendance makes this perennially one of the top three minor league clubs in the nation.

Paul Bunyan as a little boy in front of Autozone Park, home of the Redbirds

Redbirds night game at Autozone Park.

General Washburn's Escape Alley

Across the block used to be an alley that ran from Third Street to Front Street called General Washburn's Escape Alley. At Union and Main streets is a curious historical marker referring to this; it was part of the second Civil War Battle of Memphis, led by General Nathan Bedford Forrest, which had three objectives: "to capture three Union generals posted there; to release Southern prisoners from Irving Block Prison; and to cause the recall of Union forces from Northern Mississippi" *(Wikipedia)*.

Local attorney Ernest Kelly relates the story:

Memphis was under Federal occupation from the naval battle of Memphis on June 6, 1862—which is a colorful episode in its own right—until the end of the war. The only intermission in the Yankee occupation began shortly before dawn on Sunday, August 21, 1864 when Forrest and about 1,500 of his cavalry surprised the Yankee garrison, captured about six hundred of the enemy and just missed capturing Gen. Cadwallader C. Washburn (whose brother was a congressman and who, like a number of Lincoln's choices for command, was more noted for his political connections than for his military skills).

The attack was spearheaded by Forrest's brother, Captain William Forrest, who rode his horse into the lobby of the Gayoso hotel looking for Yankee generals, and by another brother, Jesse Forrest who broke into the hotel by the front door just as Washburn was making a hasty exit through the rear. Washburn had no time to dress for the occasion and hotfooted it by back alleys for Fort Pickering on the bluffs, with his nightshirt flapping in the dawn breeze. His dress uniform and some of his staff were captured. The route of Washburn's flight to the fort includes the present "General Washburn's Escape Alley."

A third general, Stephen Hurlbut, was involved in the affair. Captain Forrest had expected to find him at the Gayoso, but he was sleeping elsewhere. This aroused some scurrilous rumors as to where, but he at least arrived at the fort in proper uniform. As the previous commander, who had been sacked to make way for Washburn, he enjoyed having the last word: "They removed me from command because I couldn't keep Forrest out of West Tennessee, and now Washburn can't keep him out of his own bedroom."

Ultimately, there was a touch of chivalry to close the episode. Forrest, who had captured at least 116 Union soldiers and a couple hundred horses in the raid, met Washburn under the flag of truce near Nonconnah Creek a few miles south of downtown seeking to exchange prisoners. Washburn refused, but they exchanged clothing instead. Forrest returned Washburn's uniform, and suggested that at least Washburn could provide clothes for his captured troops, since a number of them had been caught in their night clothes as they stumbled out of bed. Washburn complied and his men were marched into captivity decently clad. Washburn hired Forrest's own Memphis tailor to produce a Confederate Gray dress uniform which he sent to Forrest.

No such chivalry graced the enemy conduct in Lafayette County, Mississippi. The main purpose of the raid on Memphis was to disrupt a powerful drive through north Mississippi by General A. J. Smith. It worked. Smith abandoned his campaign and headed back toward Memphis, but he burned Oxford before withdrawing. As an Illinois correspondent wrote, "Where once stood a handsome little country town, now only remain the blackened skeletons of houses and smoldering ruins." Earlier in the war, this would have been deplored as a criminal act. By 1864, it was part of a policy of trying to end the war by calculated atrocities against the civilian population of the South. That policy contaminated the Union government all the way to the top.

Concluding the Tour

Two more blocks north on Third Street is the First Tennessee Bank Building on Madison Avenue. Inside is a striking Tennessee mural and a historical art gallery that is worth seeing, including a captivating painting by DeWitt Jordan titled "Cotton Landing at Memphis." You can enter the building through the small door on the south side (Monroe Avenue) or the large entryway on the north side on Madison Avenue. When you exit onto Madison, walk a block west to Main Street. Just a block north is Court Square where you began the tour.

Going Downtown to Cooper-Young

This map is for both the Downtown to Midtown and Central Gardens/Cooper Young tours.

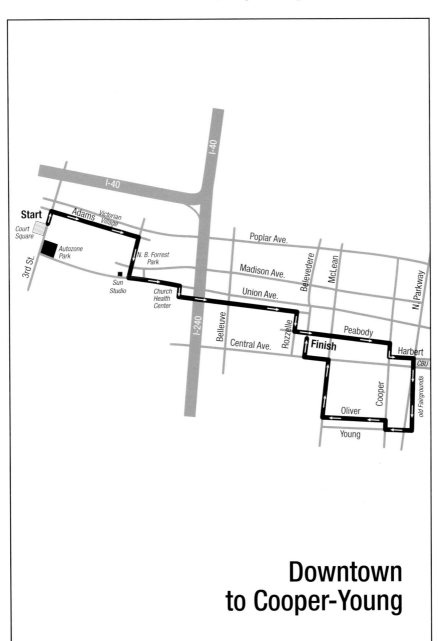

Downtown to Cooper-Young

Downtown to Midtown

The Most Controversial Walk

Begin at Court Square and Main Street.
More museums and Memphis controversy. (4 to 5 miles)

Looking for a Place to Stay...

- **Days Inn**, Union Avenue (behind the Burger King)

- **Red Roof Inn**, west side of I-240, just off Union Avenue

- **Holiday Inn Express**, east side of I-240 off Union Avenue (across from the Methodist University Hospital)

- **Gen-X Inn**, east of I-240 on Madison Avenue

The Tour

From Court Square, walk two blocks north to Adams Street. Go east on Adams Street past Calvary Episcopal Church, Saint Peter's Catholic Church, and across Danny Thomas Street.

Danny Thomas, a native Memphian and television star, was the founder of Saint Jude Research Hospital, the large buildings about a quarter-mile south of here; this is where cures for cancer continue to be discovered. Children who are patients at Saint Jude are accepted regardless of ability to pay from all over the world. It is a great source of civic pride that this world-class research hospital is located in Memphis.

Millionaire Road

Continuing east on Adams Street to Victorian Village, this was once knicknamed Millionaire Road. For around $10, you can tour the Woodruff-Fontaine House from 12 to 4 p.m., Wednesday through Sunday. Amos Woodruff, a businessman who relocated from New Jersey, built it in 1870 for under $70,000 for his complaining wife (who didn't like the Memphis heat); it was sold in 1883 to cottonman Noland Fontaine. The house is not only beautiful inside, but the doors in the dining room are thirteen feet tall.

Paul Bunyan, when he was a little boy, lived there. It was the only house in America where he didn't have to stoop over to go through the doors — up until he was twelve years old. Shortly after he hit his adolescent growth spurt no house was big enough for him, so he invented skyscrapers. In 1929, after Paul Bunyan had long moved out, the next-door neighbor Rosa Lee bought the house for $29,000 (the stock market crash had devalued it) and made it into an art school, which eventually became the Memphis College of Art (moving to Overton Park in 1959).

The James Lee Mansion is part of "Millionaire's Row" on Adams Street in the Victorian Village.

Sun Studio

At Manassas Street, turn right and walk past Forrest Park to Union Avenue. Just to the right, on the corner of Marshall and Union avenues, is Sun Studio. This is where Elvis Presley's first hits were recorded, as well as a number of other early rock-a-billy legends like Jerry Lee Lewis, Johnny Cash, and Carl Perkins. There's a very interesting museum on the second floor that you can visit for a small admissions fee.

One story from the studio was that when Elvis first came in and tried his hand at recording, Sam Phillips was about to drop him when, between sets, Elvis started playing around with "That's Alright Mama." His interpretation of the song was so unique and catchy that the band came back to their instruments, joined him, and captured Elvis' sound. It was the hit that started the train moving. From there on out, they played songs that Elvis was uniquely talented at interpreting; wherever they went, audiences were stunned with the rhythms, vocals, words, dancing, and handsomeness of this young man. Some argue that Elvis' music spawned a cultural revolution, setting the stage for the revolutions of the 1960s.

Sun Studio is a testament to the power of music to change lives. Memphis claims it is the "Birthplace of Rock and Roll." Memphis music so thoroughly shook up the world that it just may have been a major seedbed of the cultural revolutions that began in the 1960s and reached their climax in the vast number of non-violent world revolutions of 1989. Sun Studio and its spin-offs, such as Stax and Hi Records, started something much bigger than just a change in music genre.

Sun Studio at Marshall and Union streets is where Elvis Presley, Jerry Lee Lewis, and other popular performers first recorded.

Nathan Bedford Forrest Park

A block east of Sun Studios, on Union Avenue, is the Nathan Bedford Forrest Park — the most controversial park in Memphis. General Forrest was one of our nation's genius generals. Able to discern creative ways to attack over various terrains and a terrific leader of men, he, Robert E. Lee, and Abraham Lincoln are often referred to as the three geniuses of the Civil War.

However, General Forrest was also a slave trader and founder of the terrorist group, the Ku Klux Klan. Though he resigned from the Klan after recognizing its awful terrorism, lawlessness, and sadistic nature, it was still his invention... Hence, Memphis has a park honoring the founder of the KKK. For many Memphians, this is not a source of pride. For others, though, Forrest Park honors a great Civil War General and successful businessman. Every few years the debate rages on. At the very least, the park is a testament to that conflict and the passionate debate it generated.

The statue of Nathan Bedford Forrest, a Civil War General, can be found in Forrest Park. This statue is considered controversial among Memphians because Forrest was also the founder of the Ku Kluk Klan (KKK), which became so evil that Forrest himself left it.

Across the street from Forrest Park is West Tennessee State Community College. Ironically, this school is a major equalizer between the racial divide in the south, as it provides a home to many students who are able to, with the college's help, rise above the poor education they might have received in the mostly segregated public schools.

Hence, the statue of Nathan Bedford Forrest is looking at a place where the equality of all people is honored, encouraged, and made into reality. It's also a block away from the place where black and white music was fused by the genius of Elvis and other legends of Sun Studios. If that's not a testament to the incredible revolutionary nature of the South, then what is? Located side-by-side is the best and worst of human nature. Just as each person carries within oneself the capacity for hate and love, nobility and baseness, good and evil, Memphis is a city of contrasts — and this two-block section is a testament to the growing victory of goodness over the errors and narrow-mindedness of the past.

The Hospitals of Union Avenue

As you will see, within a ten-block radius is the best healthcare in the world, the center of our nation's healthcare crisis, and one of the most hopeful "solutions." This is just another example of the contrasts you will find in Memphis.

The MED

After walking through Forrest Park, continue east on Union Avenue. As you walk down the hill between the University of Tennessee Medical and Dental Schools, you will pass the site of the once massive Baptist Memorial Hospital, which was imploded to the ground in 2005 as part of the suburbanization of hospitals.

As people and money shifted to the east of Memphis, so did many of the hospitals. Not the MED (aka Regional Medical Center of Memphis), though, the county-run hospital that is just behind the U.T. Medical School. This is where Elvis Presley died, his daughter Lisa Marie Presley was born, and it houses the Elvis Presley Trauma Center. The MED is at the center of many arguments over who pays for Arkansas and Mississippi patients, revealing how Memphis is a regional force where state lines simultaneously do and do not matter.

Just north of the old Baptist Hospital site is the former location of Russwood Park, baseball home of the Memphis Chicks (short for Chickasaws) and the Negro League's Memphis Red Sox, which burned to the ground in 1960 in one of the most sensational fires in Memphis history. Just beyond that site is Methodist-LeBonheur Children's Hospital where beds are child-sized and parents are part of their children's treatment.

Wellness Center

Just past the Burger King on the south side of Union Avenue is a medical building. Walk into the driveway on the east side of the clinic just before the entrance to I-240 South. This leads you to the Church Health Center's Wellness Center, which used to be named the Hope and Healing Center, an incredible exercise and health recovery facility built and operated by the Church Health Center that began as a primary care medical clinic for the "working poor" — those who cannot afford health insurance.

The Wellness Center's mission is to attempt to change our nation's culture of physical neglect. Officials from all over the nation visit this facility and are wowed by the diversity of the people it serves, its contagious healing ambiance and spirit, and the amazing success stories of recovery, service, and help for the less fortunate. Visitors are welcome and will be given a guided tour or may simply receive a visitor's badge and walk the upstairs walking track. It's worth the visit.

The Church Health Center's Wellness Center was formerly known as the Hope & Healing Center.

Methodist University Hospital

Back on Union Avenue, heading east again, just across the interstate is the Holiday Express Inn, a nice place to stay while in Midtown. It is located across from the Methodist University Hospital, the Midtown church hospital that didn't abandon the inner city. Although it used to be the big money-maker in Methodist Health Systems, it isn't anymore — it's now a prime example of our national healthcare crisis. If you can stand the eight- to twelve-hour wait in the emergency room (unless your condition is life-threatening) and have adequate insurance, you can get high-quality care here (that might still bankrupt you nonetheless).

Though both the Methodist and Baptist Hospitals are non-profits, they are obviously run with a profit in mind, with very highly paid administrators and physicians. Unfortunately, this contributes to the ambivalence towards poorly insured or uninsured patients. Healthcare in America is troublesome.

Church Health Center

Two blocks south of this hospital is the Church Health Center where the "working poor" are cared for at affordable rates. Taking seriously "the biblical call to care for the poor who are sick," Dr. Scott Morris started this clinic in 1987, with eleven patients referred from the MED Emergency Room, across the street from the socially active St. John's United Methodist Church in cooperation with — and receiving support from — Central Church (then in Hickory Hill) and Methodist hospitals. Now supported by hundreds of local congregations, thousands of people, and even synagogues (who speak of making the world a better place for all), the Church Health Center is a national model for health care for the poor and the promotion of healthy bodies and spirits for all people.

The Church Health Center with Central High School shown in the background.

Today the Center has treated over 50,000 patients, has dental, optometry, and pastoral counseling, psychiatry, and access to over four hundred local specialists who volunteer their services. People from all over the nation visit this clinic to see how to create similar faith-based clinics in their own cities and towns. The Memphis Plan, a sort of insurance plan administered by the Church Health Center, is part of the model used by the Cover Tennessee Health Care Plan.

Concluding the Tour

A block south of this hospital is Central High School, Memphis' original high school, still referred to by its students and staff as "The High School." Like all Memphis high schools, it's the only one in the city where students are not stuck up, the morale is high yet the problems are worse than ever, and the students and faculty are demoralized but great.

Continuing east on Union Avenue, turn right onto Cleveland Street, walk a block, and then make a left onto Eastmoreland Avenue. A block away is the former home of First Congregational Church, which is across the street from the 19th Century Club, a historically philanthropic organization. The parking lot between the two buildings, owned by the 19th Century Club, was off limits to parishioners of First Congo, as it is affectionately called, because they were accepting of gays and lesbians. Now First Congo is in the Cooper-Young district, where they own their own parking lot.

Eastmoreland continues for about a half-mile to Rozelle Street; turn right (south) and walk to Peabody Avenue. Turn left onto Peabody; a block away is Belvedere Street, where you will begin the Central Gardens/Cooper-Young tour.

Central Gardens / Cooper-Young

Begin at Belvedere and Peabody avenues, next to Grace-St. Luke's Episcopal Church. Residential walking. (4.5 miles)

The Tour

Grace-St. Luke's Episcopal Church has a beautiful sanctuary with stained glass windows from a local artist and is a particular source of pride to this socially active congregation. Walk about a mile eastward, past Boss Crump's old home (marked by a historical marker) on the north side of the street. Crump was mayor for awhile, after which he continued to have his hand in many facets of city government and commerce for years — hence, the "Boss" nickname.

Mayor Crump, U.S. Representative Harold Ford Sr., and Mayor Willie Herenton are perhaps the three most influential leaders in Memphis' history, presiding over years of public service. Crump was the de factor boss of Memphis for about forty years, strong-arming people into following his recommendations. Ford was a most articulate spokesperson for the emerging black community during the 1970s and 80s (followed by his just as articulate son, Harold, Jr.). Herenton won election as Mayor in 1992 by 147 votes and served for seventeen years. He was the first African American Mayor of Memphis, and quickly established himself as a strong leader. His terms as a progressive school board executive and Mayor both ended with great uproar over his expressions of anger, self-righteousness, and sexual improprieties. Mayor Crump was the only one of these three who lived in Midtown Memphis...in a most visible and accessible mansion.

Continue east past the mostly remodeled rowhouses where the mansions' servants used to live and turn right onto Cooper Street. At the Easy Way store, turn left onto Harbert Avenue. Easy Way is a local chain that sells fresh produce year-round. It is a Memphis gem. Harbert Avenue will take you past the ballfields of Grace-St. Luke's Episcopal Church in a couple of blocks. Harbert ends with a left turn that takes you to East Parkway. When you reach East Parkway, turn right and walk south under the railroad bridge. Christian Brothers University will be on your left.

Stop at the guard station at the entrance to the Christian Brothers University (CBU); they should give you permission to explore this beautiful campus. CBU is an excellent private college that has long had a great engineering program, as well as unusual coursework like Peace Studies. It housed the Gandhi Center for Nonviolence, which was founded by the great Mohandas K. Gandhi's grandson, Arun Gandhi, a former resident of Memphis, in the early 1990s. Part of the Gandhi Center's legacy is the continuation of a nationally recognized Gandhi-King Peace Conference held in the fall of every year and now run by the Mid-South Peace and Justice Center.

The Stritch Retreat Center Chapel and garden is located on the campus of Christian Brothers University.

Stritch Center

On the northeast corner of the campus is a quaint, peaceful retreat center — the Stritch Center. It has meeting and eating rooms, a chapel, and small rooms with a single bed and a desk or, in other words, monastic-like cells. Retreat participants are often awakened with a knock on the door and a voice calling out "Christ has risen," to which the awakened retreater is expected to reply, "He is risen, indeed!"

Near the Stritch Center are the CBU baseball field, soccer field, and track. The CBU soccer and baseball teams have recently become national powers. End your CBU trek at the large parking lot south of the campus, exiting at the gatehouses.

Concluding the Tour

Now, cross Central Avenue and take the flag-lined street into the Liberty Bowl area. Just beyond the first athletic field is the site of the former Tim McCarver Stadium where the Memphis Chicks played for years until the Redbirds came to town and built the new downtown stadium. The Tim McCarver Stadium was torn down in 2003. As a result, Tim McCarver, the former baseball player and renowned baseball announcer, has nothing named after him. People wonder if he'll ever recover from this tragedy — well, at least one person does. This large tract of land is currently being redeveloped.

Walking south, you'll come to Tiger Lane, a tailgating green for Liberty Bowl games, which opened this year — forty years ahead of schedule. Maybe the other plans will be accomplished more quickly than expected. Walk west on Tiger Lane to East Parkway South.

Cooper-Young District

Go left on East Parkway and then turn right (east) on Young Avenue at the BP gas station. Young will take you to Cooper Avenue in a half-mile. This is the Cooper-Young intersection, a hot nightspot with great dining, music, dancing, and, locals complain, drunks relieving themselves in alleys.

A block south is First Congregational Church, which just may be the most left-wing church in Memphis. Inside the sanctuary is one of the most beautiful Labyrinths in the city, inlaid in the wooden floor. Ring the doorbell next to the ramped entrance on the east side of the church and they will probably let you see the Labyrinth and sanctuary.

Walking north on Cooper Avenue on the east side of the street is Burke's Bookstore, a Memphis landmark for many years.

One block north of Cooper is Oliver Avenue. Turn left and walk west on Oliver. This is typical Cooper-Young residential housing.

Turn right (north) on McLean Avenue and walk under the railroad trestle to Central Avenue. Turn left (west) on Central and walk past some of Memphis' oldest mansions. At the Catholic Church of the Immaculate Conception, whose beautiful sanctuary is often open for visitors to view (enter from the door on the west side of the sanctuary), turn right onto Belvedere Street, a 75-year-old boulevard filled with flowering trees — it just may be the most gorgeous street in Memphis each spring. Take Belvedere to Peabody Avenue; this is the corner where you began the tour.

Ceiling in sanctuary of Immaculate Conception Church, midtown

This map is for both the Overton/Evergreen
and VECA Greenway tours.

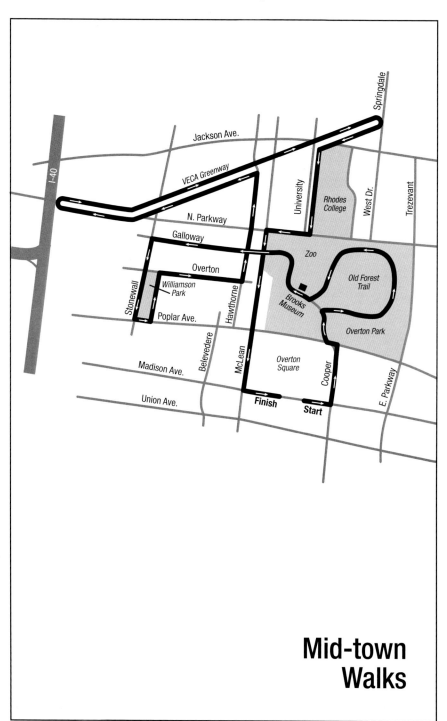

**Mid-town
Walks**

The Midtown Tour

Overton/Evergreen

Begin at Overton Park and Poplar Avenue. Urban Old Growth Forest, the Zoo, art museum, and more residential charm. (4 miles)

The Tour

Note: This walk begins in Overton Park where there is usually ample parking. If you plan to include visiting the zoo, use the zoo parking lot, which costs $3.

Rembert Street cuts across Madison or Union Avenue just east of McLean Street. Going north on Rembert takes you to the west entrance of Overton Park. Just inside the park, walk past the Memphis Brooks Museum of Art (or stop and see its excellent collection of art).

This is the oldest fine art museum in Tennessee. Opened in 1916, it was founded from a donation made by Mrs. Bessie Vance Brooks in honor of her husband and was expanded in 1983.

Since 1961, this Spring, Summer, Fall sculpture by Wheeler Williams has been in front of the Brooks Museum of Art in Overton Park.

Levitt Shell

Behind the Museum is the Overton Park Shell, named the Levitt Shell, where Memphians gather for concerts, theater, and public events — Elvis once performed here. Follow the signs to the Memphis Zoo. *(Note: The zoo costs around $15 to visit, which is recommended at the end of this walk, for you will return here in about an hour. It's a Memphis gem, and on hot summer days, it has lots of places to cool off from the walk, including places to eat.)*

From the zoo walk west on Galloway Avenue, which leaves the park next to the zoo. Continue west to Stonewall Street, which contains many large old mansions and new homes built since the I-40 corridor was resold and redeveloped. An interesting sidenote: In the 1970s a landmark court case traveled all the way to the Supreme Court where the Federal Government argued it had the right to pave I-40 right through Overton Park. Local Memphis neighbors argued against it because the park was registered as a historical site. The Supreme Court ruled in favor of the neighbors and I-40 had to find a route around most of Memphis.

Right:
Levitt Shell at Overton Park.

Hence, I-40 turns sharply north and south at Bellevue Street and, combined with I-240, splits the city in two places: next to the Wolf River to the north and the Nonconnah Creek to the south. Because of this ruling, Overton Park did not become a park split by a freeway, something Midtowners are quite happy about.

Walking south on Stonewall Street, turn left (east) on Poplar Avenue and walk one block to Williamson Park; this was once the grazing and exercise area for the horses that worked for the houses on Stonewall (the stables backed onto it). Turn left on the street that enters the park. If you walk north on the grass, you'll end up on Willett Street, a lovely neighborhood of new homes and beautiful lawns. Walk a block to Overton Park Avenue, turn right (east), and return to Overton Park. When you get to Overton Park, take the sidewalk to the southeast towards the War Memorial, which honors all of the twentieth and twenty-first century local war dead and is the place where peace rallies are often held. Funny how peace and war collide.

Overton Walking Paths

Pass the War Memorial and turn south in front of the Memphis College of Arts, a building that was designed by the same men, Bill Mann and Roy Harrover, who designed the Memphis International Airport Terminal. It was meant to look like champagne glasses, perhaps an allusion to the oft-mentioned quip that in Memphis there is a bar and a church on every corner. Well, maybe it alludes to the bar part, or maybe there was some other strange reason. Continue south to the golf clubhouse on the crushed gravel path that turns left between the first and seventh holes of the golf course (east) and into the woods.

The golf course was built in 1906 (the clubhouse in 1926) and is a nine hole par 34 course. There are a number of legends of extraordinary scores, but the official course record

was shot in 1931 by Jake Fondren — 26. That was with hickory shaft clubs named Niblick, Mashie-Niblick, and Mashie.

One of the stories told in the clubhouse is about an old man chasing teenagers joy-riding golf carts into the Old Forest trails. Trouble was, his cart was slower than theirs, so they got away. Almost. One of the boys had given his name and address to the clubhouse manager before playing golf, so after they found the carts in the middle of the forest, they called the boy's father who did the right thing.

Behind the clubhouse, you will enter a forest oasis that surrounds most of the golf course.

These trails lead into the Old Forest at Overton Park.

In the early morning, these woods are a dog's heaven. Though dogs are forbidden to be off their leash, there is tacit community agreement that friendly dogs can roam freely before 9 a.m. Every now and then a dog causes a problem, though, and the police temporarily clamp down on people who don't have their dogs leashed. Thus, early morning dog owners are always on the lookout for officers who are called the "Dog Nazis." It is not exactly an affectionate name, but after a week of ticketing irate dog owners, they turn their eyes away and dogs roam freely again, with the owners of misbehaving dogs being a bit more vigilant.

Shortly after the bridge is a path into the woods off to the left. You can wander for quite some time in the woods — what is referred to as the Old Forest — and somewhere along the way you'll come out at the paved road circling the Old Forest.

Warning! There is a history of illicit activity in these woods during the mid-day, so straying off the crushed stone trail or inner road after 10 a.m. or walking it alone is not recommended.

Inside this old southern forest are the beautiful sounds of birds, an occasional snake, squirrels and chipmunks, and sightings of what is affectionately called (unless it ate your cat) "the Midtown coyote." Early in the morning, just at the break of day, you can often hear barred owls hooting and, if you hoot back, they will fly over to see you. Catching a glimpse of them in their silent flight, alighting on a branch above you, is an unusual blessing.

If you have a good sense of direction, all you have to do is take the road west and it will lead you back to the open spaces around the College of Art and the golf course. Otherwise, continue on the inner road around the woods or take the walking trail that parallels the road. When you come to the east picnic area, however, leave this circular road or trail and continue straight (north) on the street west of and next to the picnic area that re-enters the woods.

The Memphis Zoo

At the northeast corner, next to the intersection of North and East Parkways, turn west onto the old woods road to the end and then left again, passing the controversial development of the zoo. In 2008, this section of the Old Forest was cleared for the creation of the Northwest Passage exhibit, creating an uproar of protests, including slogans like "Who speaks for the trees?" spray-painted on the zoo's green fence cover. It was a public relations nightmare for the zoo. Partly in response to the protests, the zoo promised that its next exhibit in the Old Forest to the south of the Northwest Passage, to be named "Chickasaw Forest," would be low-impact and, presumably, an excellent walk.

Continue past this exhibit back to the circular road/trail and continue to the right (west). This will lead you out of the woods to another playground. Walk around the playground to the pond, named Rainbow Lake, probably because it provides such a beautiful reflection on many days. Walk around the pond, which will lead you to the eastern edge of the zoo parking lot, and in about one hundred yards, the zoo's entrance. Inside the zoo are other beautiful walks and a couple of restaurants.

The Memphis Zoo is one of the best in the country. Its exhibits are exquisite, state-of-the-art, and its size and horticulture make it manageable and affordable. It began in the early 1900s when a bear was chained by its neck to a tree, grew into iron cages, and then was radically transformed in the 1980s and 1990s into animal-friendly homes. Mostly the zoo is quiet and peaceful, but like any place where life is preserved, tragedy happens. In 2009, one of the elephants gave birth to a 200-pound calf, but on the calf's second day of life, the calf fell, and the mother, trying to help it get back up, gored it with her tusk and killed it. Zoo keepers, the public, and, most of all, the mother elephant were overwhelmed with grief. Not much gets more real than that.

The architecture of the entrance to the Memphis Zoo draws upon its ancient Memphis, Egypt, connection.

Note: The shortest connection between Evergreen/Overton and Vollintine-Evergreen is to walk west from the zoo entrance to McLean Street, turn right, and walk two blocks to North Parkway. Turn right again and walk past Rhodes College to Center Drive in Hein Park.

However, if you want to walk once more through the Old Forest, when you leave the zoo, walk southeast through the parking lot into the large open field next to the pond. Continue past the playground into the woods. Walk east to where the road forks and go left. In about a quarter-mile you will exit the park at the North Parkway entrance to Rhodes College. Turn right (east) on North Parkway, walk one block, and turn left on Center Drive in the Hein Park residential area.

VECA Evergreen Greenway Walk

Begin at Center Street and North Parkway in Hein Park. Urban canopy surrounded by residences and beautiful Rhodes College. (4 miles)

The Tour

Note: If you want to move your car from Overton Park, drive west on Galloway, turn right on McLean, right on North Parkway, left on University Street, and park next to Rhodes College on University Street. Walk south on University Street to North Parkway and then east until you reach Center Drive in Hein Park.

Beginning on Center Drive in Hein Park, walk north past the beautiful mansions. This street was once open to through traffic, but, as you will find, it ends at a sidewalk on Jackson Avenue and Springdale Street. A number of years ago there was quite a civic argument about whether or not the residents of Hein Park could limit traffic through their neighborhood when it was such a convenient short-cut for North Memphis residents. The Hein Park residents won the court case. Developed in the late 1920s, Hein Park is our first example of an upscale neighborhood that, for some strange reason, was never required to build sidewalks like middle-class neighborhoods.

Continue north on Springdale Street for 1-1/2 blocks to the entrance of the VECA Greenway. Formerly a railroad bed, it's now maintained by local residents. Enter this canopy of trees and you can walk southwest along the Greenway for a mile and a half. The first section is part of what is called the Spring Section, for it is above where there used to be a number of springs. Here you will see a tributary of Cypress Creek below you. Because of these springs, there was an encampment of troops near here during the Civil War.

The Greenway continues for 1.4 miles and ends just across the bridge over North Parkway at the old Sears Tower, an art deco building that used to house one of Sears' largest distribution centers and stores. It's been virtually empty for twenty-five years. No one knows what to do with it, although it was recently purchased with rumors of its revitalization.

From here, walk east a half-mile on the sidewalk next to North Parkway to the bridge over I-40 — where you will get a bird's eye view of the poor folks who have to drive to get where they're going. Below you, to the south, is the intersection where six people died in the early 1990s when a truck carrying natural gas struck a bridge post. The gas drifted over the interstate, ignited, and killed several people trapped in their burning cars. When the flame returned to the gas truck, the trailer took off like a rocket, landing on a nearby home and killing a child. It was a terrible, freak tragedy. It took fifteen years for this dangerous intersection to be remodeled into the safer, better flowing intersection you now see, although for some strange (read "stupid") reason they created a new bottleneck where northbound I-40 meets I-240. Maybe highway engineers don't drive.

Urban Canopy, VECA's Greenline Trail...
This oasis is right in the middle of the city.

Rhodes College buildings are made of Arkansas stone in this Gothic style architecture.
This is the Bryan Student Life Center.

Concluding the Tour

Turn around and return the way you came, re-entering the Greenway, and ending your walk on the Greenway at University Street. Turn right (south) on University and three blocks later you will come to the main entrance of Rhodes College at Snowden Avenue. They let walkers in to explore the beautiful Gothic campus. The library is particularly impressive. At the far southwest corner of the campus, within the fence, is a lovely Labyrinth. It is an especially nice place to listen to music and walk meditatively.

Labyrinths are fairly common in Memphis since an Episcopal priest in Germantown, the Rev. Susan Crawford, took it upon herself to introduce them to area congregations in the 1990s. The one at Rhodes is one of the nicest of the outdoor Labyrinths. They are ancient walks, first created to give Christians a way to take a sacred pilgrimage when they couldn't travel to Jerusalem and the Holy Land. Their configuration leads many to reflect on the difficulty and the fascination of how our lives move in uneven paths towards the inward center where we can find a connection to the divine.

To return to your hotel, walk south on University Street to North Parkway, turn right, and walk west to McLean Street and turn left (south). McLean will take you all the way to Madison and Union Avenues. However, if you prefer a quieter street and don't mind doing a little weaving at intersections at Poplar Avenue, Hawthorn Street is one block west of McLean and a very pleasant street — or you can walk through Overton Park, retracing the route that took you from the hotel to Overton earlier.

This map goes with the following tours:
Chickasaw Gardens, University of Memphis/
Audubon Park, and Galloway Park.

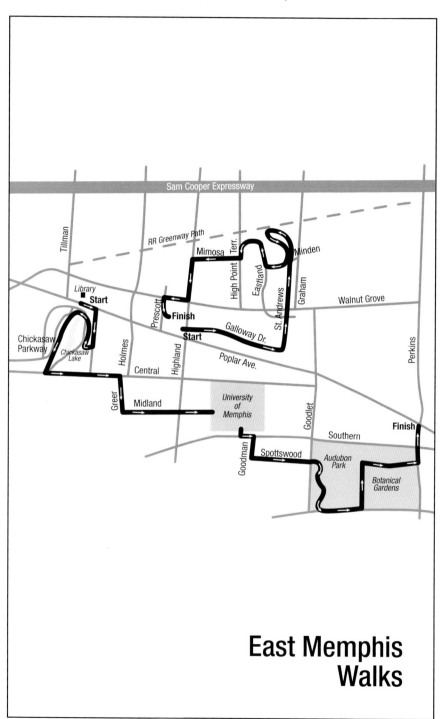

East Memphis Walks

The East Memphis Tour

Chickasaw Gardens

Beginning at the Main Library, this walk features
beautiful residences surrounding a charming lake. (3 miles)

The Tour

From your hotel, walk east on Union Avenue. It's not a very nice walk, but, hey, shouldn't you get some reminder that cities like Memphis rarely create attractive commercial districts? Idlewild Presbyterian Church, at Evergreen Street and Union Avenue, is two blocks west of McLean Street and is a particularly beautiful church and sanctuary. It is open to visitors most days (enter from Evergreen Street).

Union Avenue passes Lindenwood Christian Church and Memphis Theological Seminary. This seminary was the first southern seminary to voluntarily integrate. It is Cumberland Presbyterian, although many of its students are United Methodists and other denominations. Today, although it's not one of our nation's most prestigious seminaries, it has arguably the most diverse student body, which, in turn, creates an unusually rich learning atmosphere. It's a great place.

Continuing east, Union Avenue rises above some railroad yards. Upon crossing the bridge, stay to the right and exit on Poplar Avenue. Within about a quarter-mile is the Main Library where the walk begins.

The Main Library was built in 2000 with a striking entrance and enchanted Children's Department on the first floor. Beginning here, walk east on Poplar Avenue to the first stoplight at Lafayette Street and turn right. Walk about a half-mile to the corner of the Pink Palace Museum grounds. The Pink Palace is the former home of Clarence Saunders, the "inventor" of the self-service grocery store.

Saunders named his store Piggly Wiggly. No one knows why anyone would name a grocery store chain Piggly Wiggly, but legend is that there was a pet pig that used to roam the first store, running from excited children. Evidently when the children occasionally caught the pig, it wiggled free and they resumed the chase. Well, truthfully someone probably does know why Saunders named it Piggly Wiggly, but who wants to admit it? Today the Pink Palace is a first-class natural history museum with a wonderful movie theater. It's worth the visit.

Memphis Theological Seminary is arguably the most diverse seminary in America.

Pink Palace Natural History Museum, former home of supermarket entrepreneur Clarence Saunders

Chickasaw Gardens

Take the first right into Chickasaw Gardens at Lafayette Place. This is a curvy walk that can get very confusing, so if you get lost, Central Avenue, where you can get your bearings again, is to the south. Lafayette Place connects with Goodwin Avenue; turn right and walk a few hundred yards to Sparrow Street and then turn left. Sparrow Street ends at Chickasaw Parkway. Just across the street is a sidewalk that circles Chickasaw Lake — that's the walk you're going to take.

This area began development in the 1940s as a middle-class neighborhood, but quickly developed into upscale homes, mainly because of this wonderful, bucolic lake. Going south, circle this beautiful oasis until the lake ends on the north side at Iroquois Road or Tishomingo Lane.

Go left on either of these streets, walk to Cherokee Road, south (left) to Arawata Street, and then go east (left) to Chickasaw Parkway. Make a right (south) on Chickasaw Parkway; this will lead you to Central Avenue. Go east (left) on Central past Lafayette Street, turn left, and walk back to the Main Library *OR* continue on to Highland Street, about three-quarters of a mile away. At Highland, turn right (south) and walk a quarter-mile to Midland Avenue and the Highland Library… This is the start of the next walk.

Chickasaw Lake

University of Memphis / Audubon Park

Begin at Midland and Highland streets, near the Highland Street
Library, or near the Holiday Inn at Central Avenue and Patterson Street.
Open air park, the Botanical Gardens, art museum,
and Cancer Survivors Park. (5 to 7 miles)

The Tour

University of Memphis

Parking is difficult when the University of Memphis is in session, but there's usually a parking space available near the Highland Library on Midland Avenue, especially west of Highland Street. If you are staying at the Holiday Inn on Central Avenue near Patterson Street, just walk to the University campus from there.

Walking east on Midland Avenue to the University of Memphis campus, take any of the walks into the campus, exploring it as you wish. This is mostly a commuter school of around 20,000 students, although they're now calling it an academic and research institution. It is one of those large universities where most students do not graduate, but motivated students who carefully choose their classes and teachers can get a great education from Bachelors through their Doctorates. It's not a high prestige school unless you play on the men's basketball team — the money sport in Memphis. Native Memphians still call it Memphis State.

Right:
University of Memphis belltower

Audubon Park

End your walk through the campus on the south side and walk east on Southern Avenue, ending at Zach Curlin Street, which turns north. Cross the railroad tracks to your right (south), down to Southern Road, and continue west to Normal Street (the college was once named Memphis Normal School). Turn south and pass the athletic and alumni offices. At Spottswood Avenue, turn left (west) and walk about a half-mile to Audubon Park.

At Audubon, there is a very pleasant, curvy walking track through a nicely shaded area. Walk south to Park Avenue and continue east on the sidewalk or the golf cart path beside Park Avenue. Pass Cherry Road (which splits the park). On the right is the Dixon Galley and Gardens, a small impressive museum and garden you might want to visit. To your left, just a few hundred yards along Cherry Road, is the Memphis Botanical Garden, a beautiful, relaxing place with one of the most amazing children's playgrounds you'll ever see. It's not Kansas anymore. The artistry, design, and creative activities are fascinating. It costs about $5 to go in, but it's worth it.

Winter in Audubon Park

Cancer Survivors' Park

Walking north on Cherry Road, just beyond the Gardens, turn right onto a gravel road that will take you alongside the golf course past a small lake next to grassy fields. Keep going — you'll come to the Cancer Survivors' Park, the center of which is a labyrinth surrounded by plants, sculptures, and inspirational and informative statements.

From the Cancer Survivors' Park, walk across the field just to the north and head back to your car via Southern Avenue. Another option is to cross the railroad tracks to Poplar Avenue and walk west to the origin of the Galloway tour.

Sculpture in Cancer Survivors Park by Victor Salmones entitled "Cancer... There's Hope."

Galloway Walk

Beginning at Highland Street and Poplar Avenue, across from the
Poplar Plaza Shopping Center, this walk features golfing beauty and
more residential charm. (4 to 6 miles)

The Tour

Beginning at Poplar and Highland or one of the streets that turns off Poplar to the north after you've past Goodlett Street (if you're walking back from Audubon), walk a few blocks northwest of the Holiday Inn, at the University of Memphis, to the southeast corner of Poplar Plaza Shopping Center. *(Drivers will begin at Poplar Place Plaza, walking into Galloway Park at the corner of Poplar and Highland, and continuing east on Galloway Drive.)*

Galloway Drive

Enter this residential area by walking northeast on Galloway Drive. You will quickly come to the Galloway Golf Course, a public course that was remodeled a few years ago into one of the city's best — for a public course, that is. If you're walking early in the morning, you may walk on the grass or cart paths (not the greens). Follow Galloway Drive around the perimeter of the course to where it ends a block before Walnut Grove Avenue at Saint Andrews Fairway.

Galloway Golf Course

Memphis has a number of public golf courses with very reasonable greens fees (as low as $7 at Overton). You could spend a lot of hours enjoying these courses. Overton, a nine hole course like Riverside, is the shortest of them. Legend has it that professional golfer Jeff Sluman once posted a score in the mid-20s, which is definitely possible for a pro player. Other courses in the area are Davey Crockett in Frayser, which is the hilliest of them, Audubon, and T.O. Fuller Park.

Continue north on Saint Andrews Fairway all the way to the top of the hill where it ends at a condominium area called Saint Andrews Green. This is another upscale homes area where you can sing, "If I were a rich man…", and wonder what it would be like to live in a real mansion. Evidently, part of being rich in such neighborhoods (like Hein Park) is that you don't have sidewalks. Does that mean that rich people don't walk? Or maybe they're rich because the city doesn't make them pay for building sidewalks. Or maybe it keeps "poor" walkers out of their neighborhoods. Who knows? At any rate, by the time you stop thinking of this, you will have climbed a slight hill, and at the top of the hill it seems strangely like you are on top of a mountain…for hills in Memphis are hard to come by.

Walk back down the hill to Minden Road, turn right (west), and walk to High Point Terrace. Suddenly two things will happen. First, it becomes a middle-class area again, and, second, there are sidewalks!

Concluding the Tour

Turn north on High Point Terrace. Within five blocks is the old railroad bed that has very recently been made into a greenway path linking midtown and Shelby Farms Park. The original recommended walk allowed you to meander through local neighborhoods (shown on the map), but this path is a walkers delight and you might prefer this longer, quieter path to touring the neighborhoods. If so, turn left/west onto the greenway path. Cross Highland Avenue, where you soon are on the edge of Chickasaw Country Club, a beautiful private golf course. Continue under the Holmes Street bridge to Tillman Street where the path ends (or begins).

Turn left (south) onto Tillman Street and then left onto Walnut Grove, walking past the library, crossing Holmes, to Prescott Street at the Quaker Meetinghouse. This is the Memphis Friends Meeting, where worshippers gather in a circle and sit in silence until someone — *anyone* — feels moved to share a vocal, musical, or prayerful message. Quakers are not Amish, however, for they blend easily in our normal society, but they testify to the value of simplicity, peace, and equality. This meetinghouse moved from its long-time location in the Cooper-Young district in the fall of 2008, and its members are seeking to make it into a place where peace, simplicity, and community are accented. Just inside the fence next to the small parking area are a couple of benches where you can rest in a small beautiful garden, read some of the posted materials, and sign the guest book. Then, when the spirit moves you, continue south on Prescott Street to the Poplar Plaza Shopping Center where you began.

However, if you prefer the shorter, neighborhood tour, turn around and walk south for a half-block to Mimosa Street and take it west to Highland Avenue. Walk south on Highland to Walnut Grove Road, turn right (west), then walk to Prescott Street, turning left at the Quaker Meetinghouse, which is virtually across the street from the Poplar Plaza Shopping Center. There are a number of good, moderately priced restaurants at Poplar Plaza: La Porton (Mexican), Tasty Buffet (Chinese), McAllister's, and Buffalo Wild Wings, plus some fast food and coffee shops. Perkins, A-Tan's (Japanese and Chinese), Piccadilly, La Hacienda, and Jason's Deli are located across Poplar.

Note: You may wish to stay an extra night at the Holiday Inn next to the University of Memphis, or you might want to walk to a place closer to the next tours. Recommended is the Hampton Inn on Poplar Avenue. To get there, simply walk to Poplar Avenue (two blocks north of Central Avenue) and go east.

Quaker Meetinghouse garden

This map goes with both the Memorial Park,
Wolf River and Shelby Farms Park tours.

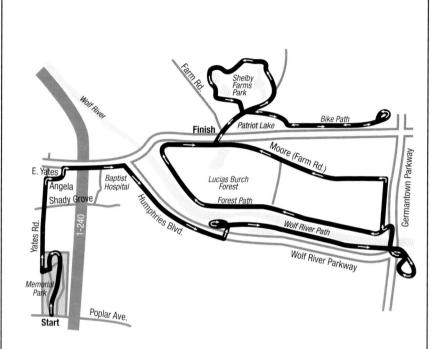

**Wolf River
Paths**

Section Six:
Scenic Paths

Memorial Park

Beginning at the Poplar Avenue entrance to Memorial Park, witness the calm, sometimes sad, beauty of a cemetery. (4 miles)

The Tour

This walk begins its scenic section at Memorial Park, which they had to build a fence around because people were dying to get in. It is open from sunrise to sunset. Memorial Park's entrance gate on Poplar Avenue is a half-mile east of the Hampton Inn, just before you get to the interstate. This is a beautiful place with a Grotto, winding paved roads, lovely memorials, and, like most cemeteries, lots of green. Explore it as long as you wish, and then walk to the west gate at Yates Street.

Memorial Park Grotto

Yates Street connects Poplar Avenue and Walnut Grove Road. Back in the early 1990s this was part of the Memphis Marathon, but its route has been changed to pass by Graceland now. You will pass by Wesleyan Hills United Methodist Church, behind which is Baron Hirsch Synagogue. This is now part of the Race for Grace, a five-kilometer run that begins two blocks north at Grace Presbyterian Church to raise funds for the Church Health Center.

You could stay on Yates Street all the way to Walnut Grove Road. If you're feeling adventuresome, though, you could take a pretty little side trip by turning right (east) just beyond Grace Presbyterian Church on Sycamore Grove Street. It will turn north and change into Grove Dale Street. About a half-mile later, turn left on Angela Street, walk one block, and then turn right (north) on East Yates Drive; this will take you to Walnut Grove. From here you may walk east on Walnut Grove, connecting you with the next walk along the Wolf River, or return to the Hampton Inn.

Wolf River

Beginning where Humphries Boulevard turns east and changes to the
Wolf River Parkway, next to Baptist Women's Hospital,
this walk features woods and river charm. (8 to 10 miles)

The Tour

Walk on the curvy sidewalk on the south side of the Humphries Boulevard/Wolf River Parkway for about two miles. You will pass the great Sequoia Tree, which is actually a *fake* tree that is a cell phone tower, the Simon Schechter School, Beth Shalom Synagogue, and the Memphis Opera House.

Right:
This giant Sequoia Tree, near the Wolf River, was transplanted by Paul Bunyan years ago; it's now disguised as a cell phone tower.

The Path to the River

Just past Kirby Parkway, you will enter the city of Germantown, and, shortly, there will be an opening in the medium where you can cross the street to a small entryway into the Wolf River Path. It begins with a half-mile loop back to the west of the bridge. You may walk that loop or head across the bridge. This peaceful trail turns east, as you walk through lush forest next to the Wolf River, for about two miles. Frogs, turtles, snakes, and herons can be welcome sights along this beautiful, paved path. This is one of the most relaxing trails in the city. The path is easy to traverse, the Wolf River flows slowly by, and the natural surprises of wildlife are nice. It's one of the best walk-and-talk paths in Memphis.

About a mile along this forest path there is a fork. Turn left over the bridge and continue east. After walking under the Germantown Parkway Bridge, the trail ends in about a half a mile. Turn back around and take the path on the west side of the bridge south and up onto the bridge. There are restaurants in this area. You will have to walk for at least a quarter-mile across the bridge to the gravel road that turns off the parkway to the left (west), where you will return to peaceful woods and fields. Across the street from here is the Bruster Ice Cream store (hint, hint). Ice cream servers just may have the only job where all the customers come in happy or are expecting to feel happy soon.

Near the Wolf River in Germantown was a nineteenth century community named Nashoba by its founder, Frances Wright, an immigrant from Scotland. She sought to create an alternative to slavery. She would buy slaves and teach them skills while they worked to earn their freedom and become productive citizens, but her idealism out-paced her pragmatism. She became a public radical, reported as the first woman to publicly speak out against slavery. Unable to achieve her utopian dream here, she, nonetheless, took her slaves to Haiti in 1830 and freed them.

A peep at the Wolf River on the Wolf River path.

The Road Not Taken?

After leaving Germantown Parkway on the gravel road, there will be a paved bicycle and walking trail. If you want to walk the next four miles in the forest, sand, and dirt, go left (south). If you want to walk in the open fields on pavement, go right (north).

The forest trail begins a few hundred yards south of the entryway. Within a quarter of a mile, you will come to a fork where you should turn left, following the yellow markers. The white markers will take you further from the Wolf River and are designated for mountain bikers. Bikers are not supposed to travel on the yellow trail.

Walk for four miles on the opposite side of the Wolf River from where you just came. This is the most rural-like trail you will have encountered with these city tours. It's a sandy loam dirt trail, easy to follow, and a serene, green, buggy, and critter abundant southern forest trail (in the summer). Like most southern forests, it's a lot more comfortable and pleasant (but not as colorful) in the wintertime. Stay on the main trail to the left.

Warning! If you are bothered by spiderwebs — they are more abundant in the early morning — take a light branch with a few twigs on it and wave it in front of you while walking to take down any webs before you barge into them.

Shortly after you pass the quarter-mile marker, take the path to the right that heads into a large clearing. The trail ends at Walnut Grove Road next to the bridge. Walking east beside the south side of the bridge, you will come to some soccer fields. Just beyond them is a stop-light where you can cross Walnut Grove and walk into Shelby Farms Park, where the next walk begins.

Cotton growing in Shelby Farms.

Another Route?

If you chose the field trail at the gravel road just off Germantown Parkway, walk on the paved path and then west through Shelby Farms, which used to be the Penal Farm, but is now mostly experimental farming and some community gardens. Southern prisons used to mostly be farms or metal shops (where license plates were made), and this large tract of land was farmed by prisoners. The prison itself is located on the northwest section of this huge urban park, but inmates are no longer sentenced to "hard labor." Now they are offered recovery and educational opportunities geared towards rehabilitation, although jails will probably always continue to be places for restraint and punishment.

The path passes bamboo fields where bamboo for the two pandas at the zoo is grown and harvested, and it turns into a rural road, back into a path, and ends at the soccer fields next to Walnut Grove. Just before you get to the soccer fields, though, is the stop-light that crosses Walnut Grove into Shelby Farms Park, the next walk.

Shelby Farms Park

Begin at Patriot Lake just inside the entrance off Farm and Walnut Grove Roads. (4 to 5 miles)

Warning! This is a very sunny and often windy walk. In summertime, it'll be *very, very* hot, except in the early morning. Be prepared with water or a wind-breaker.

The Tour

Shelby Farms Park is north of Walnut Grove Road and is also part of the old penal farm. The Shelby County Correction Center is on the west side of this farm/parkland. The largest urban park in the county, its 4,500 acres somehow have survived what has been an annual debate over whether or not to develop some of it, especially now that it is right smack in the middle of sprawling greater Memphis area.

Patriot Lake

Just east of the Walnut Grove athletic fields on the south side of Walnut Grove Road is the stoplight at the old Farm Road. Fifty yards north of Walnut Grove Road is the entrance to Shelby Farms Park and on your right is Patriot Lake with a wonderful, paved trail around it. On windy days this is a sailboat haven. Follow that trail counter clockwise. At the eastern edge of the path are dirt bike trails, named Tour de Wolf, that you can follow for about a mile to the eastern edge of the park and wind another mile or more back.

If you choose to keep walking on the Patriot Lake path, stay on it until you are just about all the way around. There you will find a short walk up to the Visitors' Center. Just north of the Visitors' Center is a paved road leading up to the hill. Breaking off that road are two more paved trails: the first one goes down a hill into some woods; the second one is relatively flat and follows along a creek. You may take either one for they are the start and finish of a 2-3/4-mile loop trail. The following description is in the clockwise direction beginning with the first trail into the woods: Within a quarter-mile along, you will cross the main driving road and soon find yourself walking next to a pond. Back into the forest for about a quarter-mile, you will soon leave the forest altogether and wind your way past the Chickasaw Lake.

Geese in Patriot Lake at Shelby Farms Park.

The Buffalo Herd

Below, to the left, is the city's buffalo herd, which is bordered by Farm Road. Every southern city should have a buffalo herd, don't you think? These particular buffalo were the inspiration for country singer Roger Miller's song, "You Can't Roller Skate in a Buffalo Herd." (Maybe.) The trail is marked by posts painted green at the top with quarter-mile markers on them. It winds its way north and east for about 1-1/2 miles along the edge of the forest — where deer, possums, raccoons, squirrels, skunks, and snakes reside — and re-enters the woods when it turns back south. This is where many of the city's high school's cross-country races are held.

Buffalo herd in Shelby Farms Park.

119

Concluding the Tour

When the path leaves the woods again, it comes to a playground where skunks are sometimes seen in the early evenings or early mornings. (Dogs love to chase skunks, but owners of dogs don't appreciate it for some reason.) To the west of the playground is an exercise trail that winds peacefully through the woods next to Pine Lake. You might enjoy that excursion. By now, you certainly need more exercise. Returning to the green post trail, you will cross Pine Lake Drive — the path follows a nice creek back to the Visitors' Center and Patriot Lake, but read the next two paragraphs first to decide if you'd rather return via the Shelby Farms Greenline Path that begins on the northern edge of the park.

The Greenline Return

The only walks left are the three that require some transportation, so this more or less linear tour of Memphis is, sadly, over, except for the walk back to your hotel or car. There is a Hampton Inn just across the Wolf River on Walnut Grove next to Baptist Hospital, but it might be time to take the Walnut Grove bus #34 back downtown to a hotel of your choice. The bus runs every thirty minutes, beginning across from Baptist Hospital, so you will have to cross the Walnut Grove Bridge. It isn't a pleasant walk, but at least it's not that far.

However, there's another way to catch the Walnut Grove bus that includes — if you've still got the interest and energy — a wonderful walk on a paved bike and pedestrian path. This would be to walk back along the Greenline Path from Shelby Farms to the end at Tillman Street. Beginning at the northwestern edge of Shelby Farms Park, this trail was opened just as this book was being completed, but the connecting trail from the park to the Greenline Path has not been finished, so the best way to get to the Path is to walk along Mullins Station Road on the northern boundary of the park. Overlook Drive or Pine Lake Drive are the quietest connectors between Walnut Grove Road and Mullins Station, although the very heavily-trafficked Farm Road connects them as well. Once on Mullins Station, walk west until the intersection with Farm Road, where the Greenline Path begins. From here it is seven miles of flat, mostly shady, mostly quiet, walking on a biking/running/walking path to the end of the Path at Tillman Street one block north of Walnut Grove Road. Here you can catch bus #34 to downtown. The Path has all the charm of the VECA Greenway traversing the backyards of America like old train tracks have always done. Just north of the Path, on High Point Terrance, are some pleasant shops at a place called High Point Station.

At the end of this tour, you will have seen much of the center of Memphis from west to east. The three remaining walks take you to two state parks north and south, the one-time upscale area of Memphis, Whitehaven, and Graceland, and Memphis' International Airport. Tonight, though, you can celebrate having accomplished a great series of walks before embarking on tours that are, really, just icing on the cake.

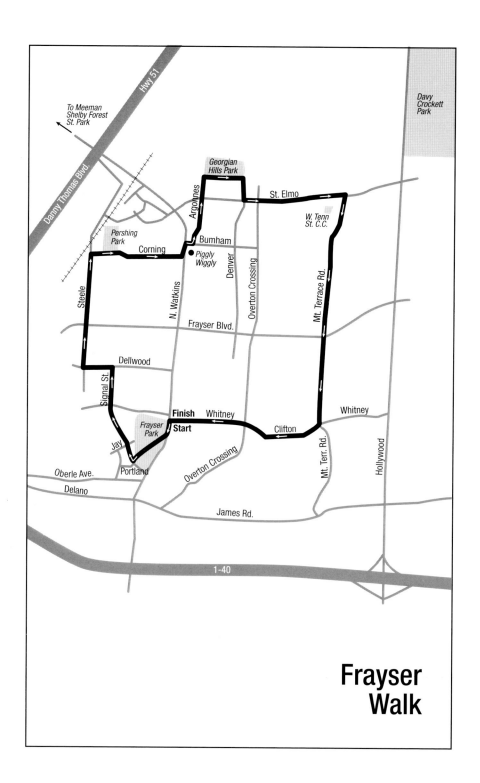

Frayser
Walk

The Urban Tour

Frayser Walk

Begin with a bus ride from Downtown to Rice Community Center.
This is a hilly residential area. (6 to 7 miles)

Warning! Many would not recommend this walk because of the high crime statistics from the area. Though this walk will not take you through obviously dangerous places, it is recommended that you walk it in the morning and follow good safety practices, as discussed in Section One.

The Tour

Travel to the Walk: From the downtown North End bus depot at Auction and Main streets, take the #10 bus and deboard at the Rice Community Center in Frayser Park at Whitney and Watkins streets.

Frayser, a working class neighborhood, has some of the prettiest terrain in Memphis. Its rolling hills and broad streets give it a charm that belies its reputation as a poor section of town. This is a simple walk that will take you through a part of the city that is underappreciated. Beginning the tour by circling Frayser Park on the walking trail — this will give you a preview of the charm of this part of Memphis.

Frayser, named after a railroad depot by that name, was originally called "The Point" because its western boundary was a peninsula between the Loosahatchie and Wolf Rivers where they emptied into the Mississippi. It grew into a major industrial suburb of the city, anchored by an International Harvester plant and the city's main airport, the General DeWitt Spain Downtown Airport. However, when International Harvester closed down in the 1970s and the new international airport was built in Whitehaven in the 1960s, Frayser became quite depressed with some high crime locales (thus, a morning walk is recommended). Nonetheless, residents often speak affectionately of the area and organize for community renovations.

Georgian Hills Park in Frayser.

Typical cute church sign in Frayser.

Piggly Wiggly

At the south end of the park, exit onto Signal Street and walk north to Dellwood Avenue. Turn left and walk to Steele Street and then go north again. After a couple of miles, turn right onto Corning Avenue. This street comes to Watkins Street about two miles north of Frayser Park. Just to the left of the Piggly Wiggly Supermarket is Burnham Street, which leads to Argonne Avenue, where a branch of the public library is housed. Turn left onto Argonne and, within one-half mile, is Georgian Hills Park, behind the Georgian Hills Schools.

Piggly Wiggly in Frayser

Take the walking trails in Georgian Hills Park and then, on the east side of the park, head back south on Denver Street to St. Elmo Avenue. Turn left and continue east on St. Elmo to Mountain Terrace Road, which is just beyond the West Tennessee State Community College. Turn right (south) on Mountain Terrance, and walk about two miles to Clifton Street. Turn right (west) on Clifton, which will turn into Whitney, and walk back to Frayser Park. Catch the #10 bus back downtown.

Though there's not much historical significance to this bedroom area of town, it is a relaxing walk.

Graceland / Airport Walk

Begin with a bus ride from Downtown to Graceland. Mostly open air, airport, and airport industry touring. (10 to 11-1/2 miles)

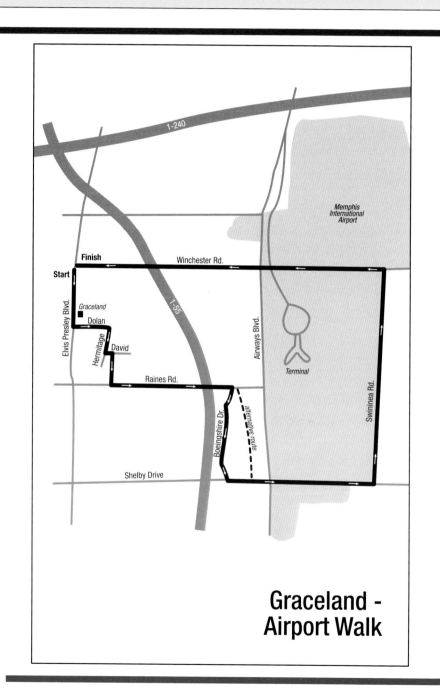

Graceland -
Airport Walk

The Tour

It is nearly a 6-1/2 mile walk from Union Avenue South on Bellevue Avenue to Graceland — and ninety percent of the walk is quite ugly and a bit on the shady side with hourly motels and suspicious places. Taking the #20 bus is recommended. It travels from the downtown North End Terminal east on Union to Bellevue and then south on Bellevue, which turns into the Elvis Presley Boulevard. Deboarding at Winchester Street, where the bus turns east, leaves you a half-mile north of Graceland. If you are driving, there are many parking places near Graceland for a fee. You can also park on Dolan Street or Favell Drive, both residential streets located just beyond Graceland (if you don't mind your car being unprotected).

Warning! Embarking on this walk on any day other than a weekend or holiday morning might cause sensory overload. Noisy with road and air traffic, it contains only a few quiet places. It is also long and traverses through a few areas that you'd be advised to avoid in the afternoons and evenings. Plus no woman should walk this route alone. However, it is part of Memphis, and it has its charm and interesting sights.

Graceland

Graceland is a mecca for travelers the world over. Thousands of them sign their names and thoughts on the stone wall in front of the mansion. There are huge gatherings here during Elvis' birthday week in January and "death week" in August. The home and two jet planes on the property are quite interesting, but at the same time a testament to the "tackiness" of the South.

The Graceland weeping wall, filled with notes from from fans the world over.

Beginning in front of Graceland, walk south less than two hundred yards to Dolan Avenue. Turn left (east) and walk one block to Favell Drive. Turn right. Continue on Favell for about 3/4-mile to Graceland Road. Turn right (south) and walk another 3/4-mile to Raines Road. Hillcrest School is at this intersection. Turn left (east) onto Raines Road and walk 1-1/2 miles to where you can see Airways Boulevard.

This begins the park-like airport buffer zone. It used to be a residential area, but when the airport expanded and grew in volume of aircrafts, it became so noisy that the airport authority was required to buy up the neighborhoods and tear down the houses. Somebody keeps the grass mowed, so you can walk the mile south to Shelby Drive weaving through the trees and former yards if you wish. It has the feel of a ghost town, so you might prefer going south on Boenshire Street to Shelby Drive.

The Memphis Airport

When you get to Shelby Drive, turn left (east) and walk for about 1-1/2 miles along the south side of the airport runways. There are sidewalks in different sections on the south side of the street, but the north side of the street has a grassy path, which is wide enough so you feel protected from the traffic and also leaves you facing traffic. Jets and turbo props will roar over your head as they land or take off. If you're fascinated with how those monstrous machines are able to get off the ground, you'll enjoy this section.

However, the traffic is unrelenting. You might have to imagine yourself walking beside a noisy ocean where the noise just never stops. Don't close your eyes, though. At least the noise is consistent. There are two spots along this section where you can stop and sit in the grass and enjoy the jets flying over — a nice, noisy experience during air traffic rush hours in the morning or late afternoon. It's interesting to see the obviously heavy Federal Express jets landing or taking off differently than the lighter passenger jets. Memphis is a hub for Delta Airlines and Federal Express. Although it's the smallest of the Delta hubs, because of Federal Express it is the busiest night-time airport in the world.

At Swinea Road, turn left (north) and walk two miles to Winchester Road. Just past Runway Street is a byrne that rises above the sidewalk. The top of the byrne is a nice place to walk, if you prefer to walk on grass. This byrne separates the airport from another residential area, and because it is somewhat sheltered, it is a favorite place for some Oakhaven high schoolers to play hooky from school.

A FedEx jet at Memphis
International Airport... the busiest
night-time airport in the world

Louisville/Memphis Rivalry

At Winchester Road, turn left (west) — you will pass the UPS facilities on one side of the street and FedEx on the other. Memphis is, of course, the world headquarters for Federal Express. Louisville, Kentucky, is the headquarters for United Parcel Services. Though these two package-toting giants are major competitors, it's only one aspect of the real reason why Memphians dislike Louis-villains. First and foremost is because the University of Louisville Cardinals sports teams have long been the grudge rivals to the University of Memphis Tigers, but since the Cardinals dropped out of the NCAA sports conference that included the Tigers (to avoid playing Memphis), the rivalry has turned all in Memphis' favor. For example:

1. Louisville lost the St. Louis Cardinals AAA Farm team to Memphis in 1998 and Memphis has turned that franchise into the number one minor league team in the nation, while Louisville's is second rate at best.

2. Louisville's once-a-year horserace that lasts all of two minutes is nothing compared with Memphis' 40+ games of professional basketball and major golf and tennis tournaments.

3. Louisville is on the Ohio River, which is but a tributary of the Mississippi River.

4. FedEx doesn't teach its drivers to be lazy and block traffic like UPS does.

5. Memphis has the Blues while Louisville claims its green grass is blue.

6. Nobody sings about Louisville, but everybody puts Memphis in their lyrics (Memphis is the #1 city in musical lyrics the world over).

7. And, of course, walking is much better in Memphis than in Louisville.

Concluding the Tour

Back to our walk: walking west on Winchester Road, you will be traveling mostly under the airport runways. It's fun to see the jets rolling over the road just in front or behind you. The underpasses are very loud places to walk, especially the second one. Winchester Road turns slightly right under a third bridge, although if you find yourself on the grassy area south of that turn you can continue walking next to the single lane and cross the access road to the airport. This road will rejoin Winchester at Airways Boulevard. From Winchester to the I-55 Bridge (about 1/1.2 miles) you will be walking through one of the more depressed areas of Memphis. (If you don't want to walk through this spooky area, catch the #20 bus, which turns north at the Elvis Presley Boulevard and will take you back downtown. If you drove, you will get off the bus a half-mile north of Graceland.)

It is sad to see this once thriving commercial district in its state of disrepair, although there are rumblings in city government and business of revitalizing it. It is trashy and ugly, and you shouldn't walk it at night. About a half-mile north of this section is Brooks Road, where prostitution and drugs are rampant, as they probably are on this section of Winchester Road, too. It's unfortunate, but still part of Memphis.

From the overpass above I-55, walk another mile on Winchester Road and turn left (south). Graceland is a half-mile away. The #20 bus will take you back Downtown.

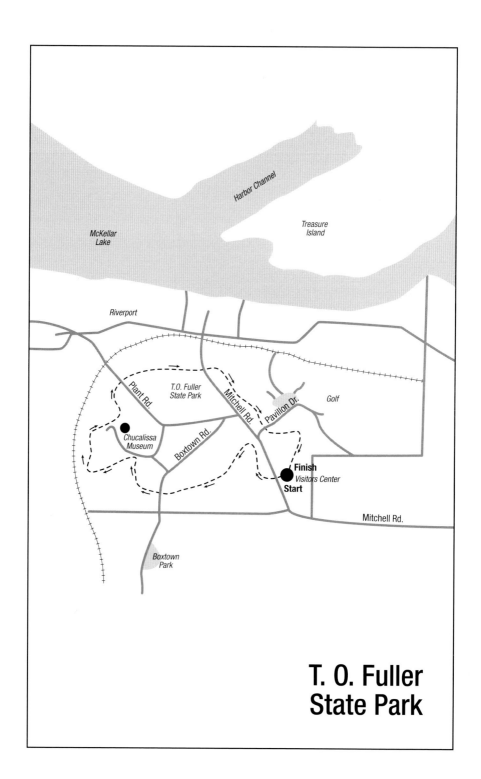

T. O. Fuller
State Park

The Park Tour

T.O. Fuller State Park

The park is thirteen miles from downtown with no bus service to it. The only way to get there is a *long, long* walk. Or drive south on Third Street to Mitchell Avenue, turn right (west), go 3-1/2 miles, and park in the lot next to the Visitors' Center. Begin the walk by crossing the street and entering at the trail head sign. If it's not too buggy, you can walk the whole six miles of the trail. One sidetrip in the park is to visit the Chucalissa Village Museum, an ancient Indian village site. (4 to 6 miles)

The Tour

T.O. Fuller State Park was established in 1938 as the Shelby Bluffs State Park for African Americans. What was then Shelby Forest State Park (now Meeman-Shelby Forest) was for whites only. It is the only state park in the City of Memphis on the southwestern edge.

Originally the land of Enoch Ensley (1835-1891), it is next to the Ensley Industrial Park and Boxtown, an area named for the poor people who built houses out of old boxcars after being displaced by the great Mississippi flood of 1927. Slaves on the Ensley plantation worked the fields just to the west of the park. T.O. Fuller was an African American Baptist preacher born on Ensley's land in 1867; he became the head pastor of First Baptist Church on Beale Street in 1900 after serving two years in the North Carolina legislature. Two years after the establishment of the park, Mayor E. H. Crump renamed it the T.O. Fuller Park.

Chucalissa Village

During the development of the park in 1940, when a swimming pool was being installed, the ancient Native American Village of Chucalissa was uncovered. Chucalissa, which means "abandoned house," is a centerpiece of the park. Now a museum and archeological project of the University of Memphis, it was a village from the 1300s until being abandoned in the 1700s when Europeans began settling in the area. The grounds used to include unearthed bones and mementos from burial grounds to view, but in the late 1980s Federal

law banned disturbance of ancient burial grounds and human skeletons. Now what you see is an interesting diorama and historical exhibit, the village grounds, and a one-half mile guided nature trail.

Like Meeman-Shelby Forest State Park, bugs are oppressive in the summertime, but this trail is fairly wide and after the first quarter-mile, you will know if you'd rather skip the trail and walk on the roads. At that point you'll be at a small clearing across the street from the entrance into the recreational section of the park.

Chucalissa (which means "abandoned house") Village grounds

137

Walking on the Roads

If you want to forego the forest trail, take that road and explore the area around the basketball courts, the swimming pool, and the picnic area. The very nice public golf course is to the east of the picnic and swimming grounds and the athletic courts. Return to the entrance road and Mitchell Avenue. Turn right onto Mitchell, now named Plant Road, up the hill to a gated "road closed" sign. Less than a half mile, this stretch of closed road is a quiet, brushy decline to a railroad bridge that is next to a bayou and lots of animals and birds.

Back up the hill to Mitchell Avenue, go right (south) onto Plant Road. Soon you come to a flat field surrounded by Crepe Myrtle. Walk through that field to the camping area. Just before entering the campground there is an iron gate next to the road to the Ranger's home. The gate leads to a grassy road that connects to a paved road, which leads to the Chucalissa Village and a picnic ground within a half-mile. It costs around $5 to visit the village. Its hours are Tuesday through Thursday 9-5 and Sunday 1-5.

Leaving the Chucalissa Village, walk back on the road towards Mitchell Street. It ends on Weaver Street, which leads west to the Ensley Industrial area and docks. However, by walking east, you will be engulfed in a beautiful canopy of trees. Weaver Street turns into Plant Road, which turns into Mitchell Street, which leads you back to where you began — 3-1/2 miles from Third Street to the east.

Forest Trail

The forest trail is six miles long, although you can shorten it in many places. The first mile and a half gives you a good idea of the terrain, plants, and beauty of the area. After that distance, you can exit at the campground or continue on the trail towards Chucalissa. You may stop there, too, and then return to the trail, which also passes next to the Chucalissa Nature Trail. The whole trail circles the park, returning you to the Visitors' Center. To see the recreational area, you'll need to exit the trail temporarily when you get to the access road.

Meeman-Shelby Forest State Park

Begin at the Visitors' Center just inside the main park entrance on Riddick Road off of Bluff Road. Hilly, soft dirt, and windy forest walks on roads. (6 to 20 miles)

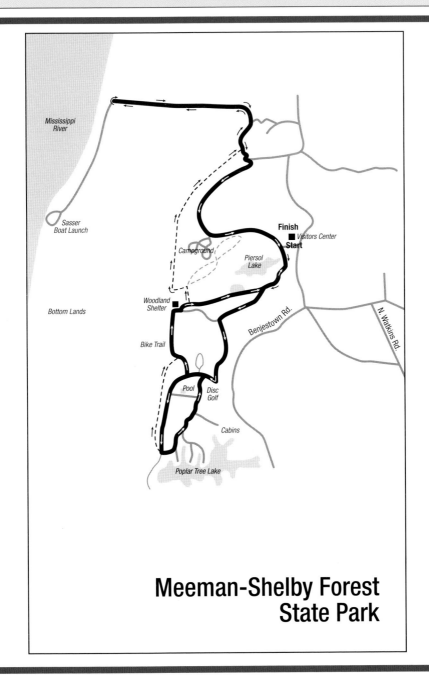

Mississippi River

Sasser Boat Launch

Finish

Visitors Center

Start

Campground

Piersol Lake

Bottom Lands

Woodland Shelter

Benjestown Rd.

N. Watkins Rd.

Bike Trail

Pool

Disc Golf

Cabins

Poplar Tree Lake

Meeman-Shelby Forest State Park

The Tour

Meeman Shelby Forest State Park is about fifteen miles north of downtown Memphis. It is a large, hilly, wooded park (13,467 acres) with miles of forest trails and winding paved roads. It is very buggy in the summer, but from mid-October until mid-April, it is a gem of a park — especially if you love hilly, soft forest trails. The hikes recommended are from seven miles (if you walk only the paved roads/bike trail from the Visitors Center and back, which is the best summer hike) to over twenty (if you walk from the Visitors' Center to Poplar Tree Lake, the whole Chickasaw Bluffs Trail, to the boat launch, and back to the Visitors Center, which is a hike best made in the winter-time).

Meeman-Shelby Forest State Park

140

The park was established in the 1940s with the help of Edward J. Meeman, a newspaper editor who also helped to establish the Great Smokey Mountains National Park. It is a beautiful park, especially in the winter. Unfortunately, the luscious green in the summer is somewhat obscured by the enormous amount of bugs — deer flies, tics, chiggers, spiders, and mosquitoes. The trails are wonderful in the late fall, winter, and early spring, but after the bugs get heavy, you have to be a hardy hiker to withstand them. That's why two hikes are recommended: one for summer that's on paved roads and the bike trail; the other for winter that includes the dirt trails.

Warning: In the summer months, take bug spray and wear light long-sleeved clothing and a hat. The deer flies, horse flies, and mosquitoes are pretty bad, as are the ticks, chiggers, and spider webs on the dirt trails. Also take along lots and lots of cold water.

Summer and Winter

Begin at the main entrance welcome center. Walk south on the main road towards Piersol and Poplar Tree Lakes. Within a hundred yards, the road drops down a steep incline to the gravel road that leads to Piersol Lake. Continue on the paved road up the hill and around the curve to a picnic area next to the small lake. There is an intersection with a "Dead End" sign to the right that actually leads deep into the woods to the Woodland Trails Shelter.

Go left, though, and walk for two miles down and up a couple of steep hills and around a number of sharp curves. This is a beautiful wooded area. Fox live under at least one of these nice bridges. This road ends at the road that comes from the back entrance to the park and the Frisbee Golf Course. Actually it's called Disc Golf, but until Baby Boomers die off it'll be called Frisbee Golf — kind of like Fritos, Kleenexes, and Xerox. Frisbee owns the brand. This is a very popular Frisbee Golf Course with some pretty incredible players gathering quite often. Turn right at the intersection and walk past the Frisbee Golf Course, continuing straight at the next intersection.

Summer

Just beyond the picnic area on your right is a bike path that you can take now or, if you want to swim (which costs about $3 and is open from 10 a.m. to 5:30 p.m. between Memorial Day and Labor Day), walk just a little further on the road to the swimming pool. Another option is to walk just over a mile down the hill to Popular Tree Lake, where you can do some boating or just relax beside the still waters. After a swim, return to the bike trailhead and take it. This path will soon begin a very steep descent down the bluffs, continuing north across the Tennessee Wildlife Recreation Association gravel road. The path then ascends back up the bluffs to the Woodland Trail Shelter. From here, the paved road that goes east (right) will lead you back to the Piersol Lake picnic area, where you can retrace your steps back to the Visitors' Center.

If you prefer to hike to the river along the paved road, walk north from the Visitors' Center towards the campgrounds. This road will wind downhill for about two miles past the Chickasaw Trailhead, down to the sharp left curve, through the farmlands, to the river.

Winter

Pass the bike trailhead and continue walking south, down the long hill past the swimming pool and a long pavilion, on to Poplar Tree Lake. The lake will be both directly in front of you and to your left when you reach the intersection where the Pioneer Spring Trailhead sign is on your right.

This beautiful little lake (much larger, though, than Piersol Lake) is a favorite fishing spot for many and has boats for rent. It is very peaceful. By now you have walked 4-1/2 miles.

After exploring the lake area, take the Pioneer Spring Trail down into the woods. It will curve to the right and continue along the river bottoms to Pioneer Spring. This trail is also the Chickasaw Trail, which will continue for 8-1/2 miles, almost to the Mississippi River at the northern edge of the park. About a half-mile past the spring, on the right, is the steep, switchback paved bike trail.

The Chickasaw Trail parallels the bike trail for about a half-mile, crossing the gravel road of the Tennessee Wildlife Recreation Association. There is a map there to help you orient yourself. If you turn to the right, you will intersect the bike trail that turns up hill to the left and continues north to the Woodland Trail Shelter.

To continue on the Chickasaw Trail, turn left and continue along the road until the trail turns off to the right. You will continue north on the Chickasaw Trail, which meanders along these bottoms — once under the water of the Mississippi River — to the paved park road. Continue on this road north until it turns sharply to the left, which, after a mile or more next to farmland, will turn back south, running parallel to the Mississippi River. Where it turns south, just to the right, is an old road that leads down to the Mississippi. Sometimes these roads are flooded with river water. If that's the case, all you can do is turn back around and head back up the park road to the Visitors' Center about three miles away.

There is no other river in America like the Mississippi: wide, deep, serene, and overwhelming at times. This sandy riverbank is home to veins of gray modeling clay. Although it is good pottery clay, it crumbles at the higher temperatures most first-class pottery clay can take, but do get your hands dirty in it. When it dries, it turns to dust and blows away when you rub your hands together (except your hands still smell a little like mold).

The return walk on the farm road past the camping area to the Visitors' Center is about five to six miles through the woods.

Afterword

Through most of this book, I've written in a passive voice. This is the second time I've used the first-person, although I've certainly expressed my opinion throughout this pilgrimage. Now, however, at the conclusion, I need to share something more personal with you, my dear readers.

I love every one of these walks. Not everyone does, which is why I've warned you about a few of them. In fact, for me, they are unforgettable. There is a natural beauty in this city that isn't as obvious as in places like Newport, Rhode Island, or Portland, Oregon, where the grandeur of the mountains or the vastness of the sea is omni-present. Sometimes it's hard to see the beauty in some places during our normal means of travel, but walking connects us to its beauty. Through my twenty-five years of walking and jogging through the city, Memphis has grown on me. In Newport or Portland there are places you can just sit down and take it all in, but in places of subtle beauty like Memphis, walking really helps.

All of my writing is about pilgrimage and sanctuaries in a way. Life is all about pilgrimage, whether it's journeying through our vocation, looking inward into our soul, seeking God, or literally becoming a traveling pilgrim. Pilgrimages are transforming — we are not the same after them because they make us grow up.

For me there is no more simple and profound way to go on a transforming pilgrimage than walking. Not only do you need very little, but as you walk, you'll find yourself realizing how much less you need than you thought you did when you started. It has been said that a necessity is a luxury you are used to. Walking is one of those ways we can naturally remind ourselves that some "necessities" are actually just luxuries we don't really need.

One of my grandest hopes for those who take this pilgrimage is that they end it with some determination to live a simpler life. What could be better than throwing off some of the complications that make our lives mad? Like the Shaker songs says, "'Tis a gift to be simple, 'tis a gift to be free."

Finding sanctuaries like these makes it much easier to live a simple life. To walk in Memphis is a simple, inexpensive delight. You need so little when you are walking. Although I wrote the book with nicer hotels and restaurant meals in mind, you can also go for the inexpensive ones and carry sandwiches if you're on a tight budget. When you're walking, luxury doesn't matter much. Simplicity is about the same for the rich or the poor. All you need, really, is a sanctuary — and the walks themselves are almost all the sanctuary you need.

Now, after nearly one hundred miles of walking, I hope you have been changed. Though you should get a certificate of achievement, what really matters is that you've done something extraordinary that has changed you. You may not know how it's changed you, but it has. Someway, somehow, you are different, but if you really need an award, why not get a t-shirt printed that says something like "I walked through Memphis." Try to explain that to your friends.

Know this, though. You are now more familiar with aspects of the city that most Memphians themselves do not know about. However, if you happen to be a Memphian, now you really know our fair city.

Congratulations, and go have some barbeque! Y'all come back now.

Index